Education Issues

Independence Educational Publishers

First published by Independence Educational Publishers

The Studio, High Green

Great Shelford

Cambridge CB22 5EG

England

© Independence 2015

Copyright

Photocopy licence

British Library Cataloguing in Publication Data

Education issues. -- (Issues ; 280)
1. Education and state--Great Britain. 2. Education--
Great Britain.
I. Series II. Acred, Cara editor.
379.4'1-dc23

ISBN-13: 9781861687081

Printed in Great Britain
Zenith Print Group

Contents

Introduction

Education Issues is Volume 280 in the **ISSUES** series. The aim of the series is to offer current, diverse information about important issues in our world, from a UK perspective.

ABOUT EDUCATION ISSUES

The world of education seems to be constantly evolving and many people worry that both staff and students are placed under increasing pressure to excel. This book examines education systems in the UK, looking at current issues and trends. It also considers how academies and free schools are changing the education landscape, and looks forward to digital innovations that could change classrooms across the globe.

OUR SOURCES

Titles in the **ISSUES** series are designed to function as educational resource books, providing a balanced overview of a specific subject.

The information in our books is comprised of facts, articles and opinions from many different sources, including:

⇨ Newspaper reports and opinion pieces

⇨ Website factsheets

⇨ Magazine and journal articles

⇨ Statistics and surveys

⇨ Government reports

⇨ Literature from special interest groups

A NOTE ON CRITICAL EVALUATION

Because the information reprinted here is from a number of different sources, readers should bear in mind the origin of the text and whether the source is likely to have a particular bias when presenting information (or when conducting their research). It is hoped that, as you read about the many aspects of the issues explored in this book, you will critically evaluate the information presented.

It is important that you decide whether you are being presented with facts or opinions. Does the writer give a biased or unbiased report? If an opinion is being expressed, do you agree with the writer? Is there potential bias to the 'facts' or statistics behind an article?

ASSIGNMENTS

In the back of this book, you will find a selection of assignments designed to help you engage with the articles you have been reading and to explore your own opinions. Some tasks will take longer than others and there is a mixture of design, writing and research-based activities that you can complete alone or in a group.

FURTHER RESEARCH

At the end of each article we have listed its source and a website that you can visit if you would like to conduct your own research. Please remember to critically evaluate any sources that you consult and consider whether the information you are viewing is accurate and unbiased.

Useful weblinks

www.cbi.org.uk

www.childrenssociety.org.uk

www.diplomatmagazine.com

www.if.org.uk

www.localschoolsnetwork.org.uk

www.ncb.org.uk

www.newschoolsnetwork.org

www.nus.org.uk

www.parentdish.co.uk

www.pcr-online.biz

www.savethechildren.org.uk

www.suttontrust.com

www.suttontrust.com

An overview of the uk primary and secondary education system

Professor T.E.A. Beravale provides a valuable insight into the sometimes daunting complexities of the UK education system.

At first glance, the UK education system can seem rather complicated to an outsider, and indeed many UK nationals face similar challenges when trying to find appropriate schooling for their offspring. Moreover, the system is subject to great change in the wake of fluctuating government policies. Although several options may be available, there is intense competition for admission to the best schools, and the financial implications of one's choice can be considerable. In this article, I will provide an overview of primary and secondary education in this country. The coalition government strongly supports independent academies, and I will explain what these are all about. I will also provide some suggestions as to where additional information can be found.

Types of schools

Broadly speaking, all primary and secondary education providers in the UK are either state or independent schools. State schools are officially known as 'maintained' schools because they rely on government funding. In contrast, independent schools – commonly referred to as 'private' schools, or more traditionally (and somewhat confusingly) as 'public' schools – receive no government funding and must therefore charge for their services. Faith schools, which are linked to formal religious organisations, are mostly – though not always – state-funded. Meanwhile, academies, introduced under the Blair government, are 'publicly funded independent schools' established and managed by sponsors from

education, business, faith or other voluntary groups. The newest addition, by the coalition government, to the education structure in the UK is Free Schools, which I will also explain.

1. State schools

State schools, as administered by local authorities, are obliged to offer free education to children within their respective catchment areas. However, in order to qualify for state schooling, a child must be deemed a permanent resident of a catchment area – a condition that may not be satisfied by the children of diplomats. Moreover, parents cannot necessarily expect to be able to place their children in schools of their own choosing. For these reasons, whenever state schooling is being considered, the relevant local authority should be approached as soon as possible.

In the state system, children start primary school at the age of five. Primary school lasts for six years, until the age of 11 (years 1-6). Secondary education is from ages 11-16 (years 7-11). Those taking A-levels (see below) stay on for two more years, until the age of 18, to complete sixth form (years 12 and 13). As of 2008, 10-year-olds entering secondary school are required to remain at school or in some other form of education – such as an apprenticeship – until the age of 18.

Maintained schools follow the National Curriculum, which is a government-determined set of standardised subjects and tests, designed to ensure that all students are taught the same thing to the same level. Compulsory

core subjects include Mathematics, English and Science. Pupils also select from a wide range of optional subjects in the last years of secondary education (the choice of which will, to an extent, define the options available for further study).

At the end of year 11, all pupils are required to sit General Certificate of Secondary Education (GCSE) exams in the core subjects as well as their choice subjects. After that, they may choose to take their A-levels, which are subdivided into Advanced Subsidiary (AS) and A2 examination modules during years 12 and 13 respectively. Some state schools now offer the International Baccalaureate (IB) diploma instead of A-levels (see p. 11). The government has recently announced plans to change the examination system, however it remains to be seen what the changes will be and when they will be implemented.

Grammar schools should also be mentioned, to which admission is decided on the basis of an entrance test, known as the 11+. (It is for this reason that non-selective state schools are often referred to as 'comprehensives'.) Academically speaking, grammar schools are among the best in the country, but they exist in relatively few counties, as their selective admission procedures have regrettably led to much opposition from national politicians as well as from local authorities.

In addition to academic studies, a wide range of vocational training is offered within the state education system.

2. Independent schools

For various reasons, often to do with quality control, parents may be inclined to educate their children privately by enrolling them at independent, fee-paying schools. Preparatory, or 'prep' schools, are for pupils aged between seven and 11 or 13. (Many of these schools also offer 'pre-prep' schooling for children under the age of seven.) Traditionally, prep schools prepare pupils for the Common Entrance Examination, a standardised test sat at the age of either 11 or 13 and used by most senior schools – i.e. independent secondary schools – as a means of determining admission, in addition to their own entrance criteria.

The best independent schools offer unrivalled quality in education. Class sizes are small, with a low pupil-teacher ratio, and although most schools follow the National Curriculum (with most pupils sitting the same GCSE and A-level exams referred to above), they often extend far beyond it, offering many specialist options in numerous subjects. (Again, a number of independent schools also follow the IB diploma programme – see below.) In addition, they tend to boast outstanding facilities for sport, art, music and so on. Good independent schools aim at providing not only an excellent academic education, but also at developing their pupils' characters and allowing them to excel wherever they show the inclination and ability.

There are also independent schools that cater to different nationalities, such as the Lycée Français Charles de Gaulle in London, which is attended by the children of several diplomats.

However, a good education comes at a price. For example, annual fees at Westminster School are £32,490 for boarders and £22,500 for day pupils (2014-15), and at St Paul's School are £32,640 for boarders and £21,792 for day pupils (2014-15). Fees for 2015-16 will be announced over the coming months.

Many independent schools started out as religious foundations and remain so to this day; nevertheless, most of them are open to children of any denomination, although some give preference to members of the faith to which the school is affiliated.

3. Faith schools

This brings us to our third category: faith schools. About 20 per cent of children attend faith schools. Most of these are run by the Church of England, but some are Roman Catholic, and a smaller number belong to other faiths such as Judaism or Islam. The vast majority are maintained schools operating at the primary level. The exception is provided by a few independent schools, most of them secondary; these include Hasmonean High School (Orthodox Jewish) in North London and Ampleforth College (Catholic) in Yorkshire.

When it comes to admissions, faith schools may give preference to members of their respective religions. This is particularly true of Catholic schools, where having at least one parent who is a communicant member of the Church tends to be a requirement for admission. Anglican schools, on the other hand, are usually willing to admit a substantial proportion of children of other faiths (or of no faith at all). In general, faith schools follow the National Curriculum, but naturally place greater emphasis on religious education than either non-denominational state schools or independent schools with more notional religious affiliations.

4. Academies

The first three academies – The Business Academy Bexley (London), Greig City Academy (Hornsey, London) and Unity City Academy (Middlesbrough) – were established in 2002. The coalition government actively promotes academies with financial incentives and has introduced legislation that will make it much easier for schools to achieve academy status. As a consequence, there has been a large increase in the number of academies, with 2,795 open in England alone as of April 2014. This includes a number of state schools, mainly at the secondary level, but also some primary schools.

As discussed above, academies are state-funded, privately run schools. They are set up as companies with charitable status. Each academy is controlled by a governing body, the majority of which is appointed by the establishing sponsor – however the principal, a local authority representative and at least one elected parent representative must also sit on the board. Governors have responsibility for the employment of staff, administration of finances, and

approval of personnel policies and procedures.

All academies specialise in one or more subject areas. (The National Curriculum has now been made more flexible to accommodate the kind of innovation that academies have fostered.) As with all state-funded schools, they are required to follow the National Curriculum in the core subjects of English, Maths, Science and Information and Communication Technologies (ICT). The overall aim of promoting academies is to provide additional quality and capacity in areas of inadequate educational opportunity and attainment: most academies either replace existing underperforming schools or meet a localised shortage in places, while a smaller number federate with weaker schools to improve the overall quality of service.

Sponsors seeking to set up an academy are expected to establish an endowment fund, capped at a maximum of £2 million, to help cover capital costs. (One exception is that sponsors from the educational sector – in recognition of the fact that they may bring value to an academy through their reputation and expertise but have limited access to charitable resources – are not required to commit any specific sum to the endowment fund.) The Department for Education, meanwhile, undertakes to cover the academy's running costs on a comparable basis to other schools in the area with similar characteristics. It should, however, be added that several successful comprehensives, as well as some grammar schools, have also applied for academy status.

5. Free schools

A variant on Academies, these all-ability state-funded schools are set up by individuals in response to the educational needs of their community. For instance, the West London Free School established by author Toby Young (*How to Lose Friends and Alienate People*) aims to provide academic excellence through a classic education. For example, Latin is a compulsory subject up to age 14, and a house structure and big emphasis on sport foster a competitive atmosphere. Admission is decided by local councils and the school

governing body and applications, as with any maintained school, are made through the Common Application Form. Schools are subject to the same inspections by Ofsted, the school regulator, as all other schools.

The International Baccalaureate (IB)

Britain has recently experienced an increase in the popularity of the IB. The IB diploma is currently offered by 155 schools and colleges in Britain. Of schools offering the IB, two thirds are state-funded. It is believed that demand will continue to grow as schools take advantage of the coalition government's advocacy of academies, which enjoy greater freedom over setting their curricula.

The IB diploma is assessed after two years of study. It is much broader than the A-level programme, with students choosing six subjects – three at 'higher' and three at 'standard' level – including English, Maths, a science and a second language. In contrast, A-levels offer a much higher degree of specialisation – a choice between the two systems therefore needs to take into account the interests, development and future aspirations of the pupil.

For the children of diplomats who may not complete their secondary or sixth-form education in London, the IB may allow for an easier transfer back to their home country (or to another posting), provided a place can be found at another school that offers the IB diploma.

School rankings

Schools in the UK are ranked according to their pupils' examination results. Official School League Tables for state and independent schools can be accessed online.

These tables show the most current GCSE and A-level results for state and independent schools in England, listed in descending order. League tables for state-run primary schools can also be found at the same site; unfortunately, a comprehensive ranking of fee-paying preparatory schools is not available, since a third of them do not enter their pupils for the relevant standardised tests.

School league tables only present part of the picture of a school's overall achievements. The inspection reports produced by Ofsted provide another useful source of information and can be accessed online at www.ofsted.gov.uk/inspection-reports/find-inspection-report. Visits to prospective schools, to meet with teachers and pupils and to inspect facilities, are also strongly recommended.

Summary

Many variables will have an impact on which education provider one eventually chooses for one's child, whether at the primary or secondary level. These include where the family lives, the availability of appropriate schools nearby, the quality of education and extra-curricular activities offered by a prospective school, and the costs of attending an independent school. As I have pointed out in this article, much relevant information is available online and from visits to the schools themselves. To this end, it is finding the right balance of academic and social experience that will determine the best choice for a particular pupil. Such a balance is ultimately personal, as what matters most is that the pupil be encouraged to develop his or her talents to the fullest.

Professor Beravale is grateful to Mr A.C. Graham, former Headmaster of Mill Hill School and House Master at Eton, and Mrs Graham, former Head of German at North London Collegiate School and teacher at Queen's College in Harley Street – a school much frequented by the children of diplomats – for their valuable comments and suggestions.

Spring 2015

⇨ The above information is reprinted with kind permission from Diplomat magazine. Please visit www.diplomatmagazine.com for further information.

The national curriculum

1. Overview

The 'basic' school curriculum includes the 'national curriculum', as well as religious education and sex education.

The national curriculum is a set of subjects and standards used by primary and secondary schools so children learn the same things. It covers what subjects are taught and the standards children should reach in each subject.

Other types of school like academies and private schools don't have to follow the national curriculum. Academies must teach a broad and balanced curriculum including English, maths and science. They must also teach religious education.

Key stages

The national curriculum is organised into blocks of years called 'key stages' (KS). At the end of each key stage, your child's teacher will formally assess their performance to measure your child's progress.

Assessments

The school must report your child's progress to you. This can happen in different ways, e.g. an end-of-term report or meetings at the school.

Children will start sitting the new national primary curriculum tests in 2016.

Children in Years 2 and 6 will be the last to receive an end-of-key-stage 'level', in summer 2015.

2. Key stage 1 and 2

Compulsory national curriculum subjects at primary school are:

⇨ English

⇨ maths

Age	Year	Key	Assessment	Average level of attainment
3–4		Early years		
4–5	Reception	Early years		
5–6	Year 1	KS1	Phonics screening check	
6–7	Year 2	KS1	Teacher assessments in English, maths and science	2
7–8	Year 3	KS2		
8–9	Year 4	KS2		
9–10	Year 5	KS2		
10–11	Year 6	KS2	National tests and teacher assessments in English, maths and science	4
11–12	Year 7	KS3	Teacher assessments	
12–13	Year 8	KS3	Teacher assessments	
13–14	Year 9	KS3	Teacher assessments	5/6
14–15	Year 10	KS4	Some children take GCSEs	
15–16	Year 11	KS4	Most children take GCSEs or other national qualifications	

⇨ science

⇨ design and technology

⇨ history

⇨ geography

⇨ art and design

⇨ music

⇨ physical education (PE), including swimming

⇨ information and communication technology (ICT)

⇨ ancient and modern foreign languages (at key stage 2).

Schools can develop their own ICT curricula or follow the programmes of study. They must also provide religious education (RE) but parents can ask for their children to be taken out of the whole lesson or part of it.

Schools often also teach:

⇨ personal, social and health education (PSHE)

⇨ citizenship

⇨ modern foreign languages (at key stage 1).

Tests and assessments

Year 1 phonics screening check

The check will take place in June when your child will read 40 words out loud to a teacher. You'll find out how your child did, and their teacher will assess whether he or she needs extra help with reading. If your child doesn't do well enough in the check they'll have to do it again in Year 2.

Key stage 1

Key stage 1 tasks and tests cover:

⇨ reading

⇨ writing

⇨ speaking and listening

⇨ maths

⇨ science.

The tasks and tests are taken when the school chooses.

Your child's teacher will use the child's work (including spoken work and homework) to work out what level your child is at in each area.

You can ask for the results but they're only used to help the teacher assess your child's work.

Key stage 2

Key stage 2 tests cover:

⇨ English reading

⇨ English grammar, punctuation and spelling

⇨ maths (including mental arithmetic).

The tests are taken in mid-May and last under five hours 30 minutes in total. You'll get the results in July. If your child is demonstrating higher achievement then the headteacher may put them in for extra tests.

When your child reaches the end of key stage 2 the teacher will also report on your child's progress in English, maths and science.

3. Key stage 3 and 4

Key stage 3

Compulsory national curriculum subjects are:

⇨ English

⇨ maths

⇨ science

⇨ history

⇨ geography

⇨ modern foreign languages

⇨ design and technology

⇨ art and design

⇨ music

⇨ physical education

⇨ citizenship

⇨ information and communication technology (ICT).

Schools can develop their own ICT curricula or follow the programmes of study.

They must also provide religious education (RE) and sex education

from key stage 3 but parents can ask for their children to be taken out of the whole lesson or part of it.

Key stage 4

During key stage 4 most pupils work towards national qualifications – usually GCSEs.

The compulsory national curriculum subjects are the 'core' and 'foundation' subjects.

Core subjects are:

⇨ English

⇨ maths

⇨ science.

Foundation subjects are:

⇨ information and communication technology (ICT)

⇨ physical education

⇨ citizenship.

Schools must also offer at least one subject from each of these areas:

⇨ arts

⇨ design and technology

⇨ humanities

⇨ modern foreign languages.

They must also provide religious education (RE) and sex education at key stage 4.

English Baccalaureate (EBacc)

In performance tables, the EBacc shows how many students got a GCSE grade C or above in English, maths, two sciences, a language, and history or geography.

4. Other compulsory subjects

Children must also study:

⇨ sex and relationships education (Year 7 onwards)

⇨ religious education (RE).

They may not have to take exams in these subjects.

Sex and relationship education

Sex and relationship education (SRE) is compulsory from age 11 onwards. It involves teaching children about reproduction, sexuality and sexual health. It doesn't promote early sexual activity or any particular sexual orientation.

Some parts of sex and relationship education are compulsory – these are part of the national curriculum for science. Parents can withdraw their children from all other parts of sex and relationship education if they want.

All schools must have a written policy on sex education, which they must make available to parents for free.

Religious education

Schools have to teach RE but parents can withdraw their children for all or part of the lessons. Pupils can choose to withdraw themselves once they're 18.

Local councils are responsible for deciding the RE syllabus, but faith schools and academies can set their own.

12 February 2015

⇨ The above information is reprinted with kind permission from GOV.UK. Please visit www. gov.uk for further information.

What's the difference between GCSEs and IGCSEs, A-levels and IB?

By Glynis Kozma

The summer term at secondary school means one thing to pupils in Years 11 to 13: exams. Until recently pupils were entered for either GCSE or A-level examinations, with A-levels divided into two levels: AS at the end of Year 12 and A2 at the end of Year 13.

But, nothing stays the same in the examination system: you may remember that in 1988 the GCSE exam replaced the former 'O' Level and CSE exams, and coursework for GCSEs was introduced for the first time.

Since then there has been much debate about the value and structure of the current exams. The outcome: further changes have been made to the balance of coursework and final exams. If that isn't enough for parents – and schools – to contend with, there are two other examinations available for pupils: the International GCSE (IGCSE) and the International Baccalaureate (IB).

So what are the differences and, if you do have any choice, which might suit your child best?

Before looking at the differences between these qualifications, it's worth understanding that you may have no choice: some schools offer both, but if your heart is set on your child studying for IGCSE or the IB you may have to change schools, particularly at 16 for the IB.

GCSE

Until 2013, the GCSE exam consisted of coursework – sometimes referred to as 'controlled assessment' – and exams. A review by Ofqual in 2013 concluded that the coursework element of GCSEs should be scrapped except, for example, in some subjects including science where experiments could demonstrate pupils' knowledge. The emphasis now is for exams to be linear – that is with one final exam – rather than modular – the previous structure which allowed pupils to

be assessed on smaller chunks of learning across two years.

GCSE exam grades are currently A*–G but these are due to change and are likely to be replaced with Grades 1–9.

At present, some exams are two-tier, so pupils can be entered for the higher or foundation tiers with their final grade being determined by the tier. For example, at foundation level a Grade C may be the maximum.

The GCSE course is usually two years but some schools will allow more able pupils to complete it in one year, or take the exams a year earlier. The majority of the exams are in June, with re-sits taken in November.

Pupils are no longer able to take English and Maths exams in November as their first entry, only for re-sits. Although some exam boards will still offer modular GCSE courses, from 2015 only linear courses will be accepted as qualifications in England.

So, to sum all of that up:

⇨ Recent changes to the current GCSE exams mean that coursework is reduced to the absolute minimum.

⇨ Most pupils are assessed by a final exam(s) at the end of two years rather than more frequent assessments over their course.

⇨ Grades will change from A*–G and be replaced with Grades 1–9.

IGCSE

The International GCSE was first introduced around 25 years ago so that pupils overseas, whose first language was not necessarily English, could take the exam. The syllabus includes many elements that are now not in the revised GCSE – mainly coursework.

Assessment takes place at the end of the course and includes written, oral, coursework and practical assessment. Grades are the same as for GCSEs A*–G.

The subjects which can be studied are the same as for GCSE but also include many foreign languages.

Many independent schools now enter pupils for this exam – possibly because they have many pupils from overseas whose first language is not English – and also because a large number of schools were disappointed at how the GCSE English exam was marked in recent years with controversy over grade boundaries.

What are the differences between GCSE and IGCSE exams?

The main difference is that the IGCSE still includes some elements of the old GCSE: coursework, oral and practical assessment as well as exams. The IGCSE is offered at different levels, and some teachers think that it has more scope for more able pupils at the higher level.

But opinions on GCSE and IGCSE exams are mixed: many more state schools are entering their pupils for the IGCSE exam because they prefer the mix of coursework and exams which is now no longer so evident in the new GCSE curriculum. There is also more scope for teachers to choose from a wider range of material.

Last year (2013), 78,000 pupils took the IGCSE English language exam compared with 17,000 a year ago. Some school enter pupils for both exams.

Some teachers – and pupils – think that the IGCSE exam is now easier than the new GCSE exam, because of the content of the syllabus and the range of assessment.

As a parent, it is probably unlikely that you will be able to choose which exam your child is entered for. If the school offers both, then discuss your child's needs. If your child achieves higher marks with coursework and performs badly under exam conditions, then the IGCSE is an option.

But be aware that some universities have their own preferences. An increasing number are happy to accept International GCSE English, but some will not.

If your child is heading for university you should, even at this stage, research entry requirements on each university's website.

A-levels

From 2015, A-levels (also known as A2) will change in ways similar to GCSEs:

⇨ They will be linear and not modular.

⇨ The exam will be at the end of the two-year course.

⇨ AS levels which used to form the first year of a full A-level course will no longer do so.

⇨ AS levels will exist as standalone courses, but they will not form part of an overall A2 grade.

⇨ The changes will take effect in 2015 for most subjects but not until 2016 for maths and modern languages.

AS courses give pupils a broader understanding of a subject but not as much as a full A-level. Most pupils will study three and possibly four A-levels.

International Baccalaureate

If your child's school offers an alternative to A-levels, it is likely to be the International Baccalaureate (IB or IBac). Developed in 1968 in Switzerland the IB has become very popular, especially with independent schools. It is highly regarded by universities. International Baccalaureate is available at several levels but the one which applies to students aged 16–19 is the IB Diploma.

This is how the IBO describes the course:

The IB Diploma

The Diploma Programme prepares students for effective participation in a rapidly evolving and increasingly global society as they:

⇨ develop physically, intellectually, emotionally and ethically

⇨ acquire breadth and depth of knowledge and understanding,

studying courses from six subject groups

⇨ develop the skills and a positive attitude toward learning that will prepare them for higher education

⇨ study at least two languages and increase understanding of cultures, including their own

⇨ make connections across traditional academic disciplines and explore the nature of knowledge through the programme's unique theory of knowledge course

⇨ undertake in-depth research into an area of interest through the lens of one or more academic disciplines in the extended essay

⇨ enhance their personal and interpersonal development through creativity, action and service.

What does the IB Diploma include?

Unlike A-levels which focus on three or four main subjects, the IB Diploma includes six groups of subjects.

IB Diploma Programme students must choose one subject from each of five groups (1 to 5), ensuring breadth of knowledge and understanding in their best language, additional language(s), the social sciences, the experimental sciences and mathematics. Students may choose either an arts subject from group 6, or a second subject from groups 1 to 5.

At least three and not more than four subjects are taken at higher level (240 teaching hours), while the other subjects are taken at standard level (150 teaching hours). Students can study and take examinations, in English, French or Spanish.

In addition to disciplinary and interdisciplinary study, the Diploma Programme features three core elements that broaden students' educational experience and challenge them to apply their knowledge and skills.

How is the Diploma graded?

⇨ The overall grade is a total of all the key areas studied – not each separate subject.

⇨ Students are awarded a grade from 1–7 for each of the six key subject areas.

⇨ In addition, three marks are available for certain parts of the course, making a possible total of 45 marks.

⇨ The pass mark is 24 as long as a minimum number of marks is achieved across each part, along with a satisfactory level of achievement on creativity, action and service (CAS).

⇨ The Diploma has a success rate of 80 per cent with less than one per cent of students achieving 45 marks.

Why would my child want to choose the IB Diploma?

The IB Diploma provides an opportunity to study several subject areas in depth as well as focusing on personal development alongside academic study. This can be attractive to pupils who find it hard to choose only three or four A-level subjects and who don't want to specialise too early.

Delaying specialisation means there are more degree options available for longer, if your child isn't sure about what they want to study at university – which many 16-year-olds aren't!

The disadvantage of the IB is that it is a demanding workload and some pupils will have to work very hard to maintain and achieve good grades across each subject area if they have strengths and weaknesses. It's maybe best suited to highly-able 'all rounders'.

Further information can be found at:

⇨ www.ofqual.gov.uk

⇨ www.gov.uk/dfe

⇨ www.cie.org.uk

⇨ www.ibo.org

⇨ The above information is reprinted with kind permission from Parent Dish. Please visit www.parentdish.co.uk for further information.

© 2015 AOL (UK)

Hard evidence: at what age are children ready for school?

An article from The Conversation.

By David Whitebread, Senior Lecturer in Psychology and Education at the University of Cambridge

THE CONVERSATION

When are children 'ready' for school? There is much debate about when the transition between play-based pre-school and the start of 'formal' schooling should begin. The trend in the UK primary school curriculum over recent decades has been towards an earlier start to formal instruction, and an erosion of learning through play.

But the evidence from international comparisons and psychological research of young children's development all points to the advantages of a later start to formal instruction, particularly in relation to literacy.

Among the earliest in Europe

Children in England are admitted into reception classes in primary schools at age four; in many cases, if their birthdays are in the summer months, when they have only just turned four. This is in stark contrast to the vast majority of other European countries, many of which currently enjoy higher levels of educational achievement. In Europe, the most common school starting age is six, and even seven in some cases such as Finland.

From the moment children in England enter the reception class, the pressure is on for them to learn to read, write and do formal written maths. In many schools, children are identified as 'behind' with reading before they would even have started school in many other countries. Now the Government is introducing tests for four-year-olds soon after starting school.

There is no research evidence to support claims from government that 'earlier is better'. By contrast, a considerable body of evidence clearly indicates the crucial importance of play in young children's development, the value of an extended period of playful learning before the start of formal schooling, and the damaging consequences of starting the formal learning of literacy and numeracy too young.

Importance of play

A range of anthropological studies of children's play in hunter-gatherer societies and other evolutionary psychology studies of play in the young of mammals have identified play as an adaptation which evolved in early human social groups, enabling humans to become powerful learners and problem-solvers.

Some neuroscientists' research has supported this view of play as

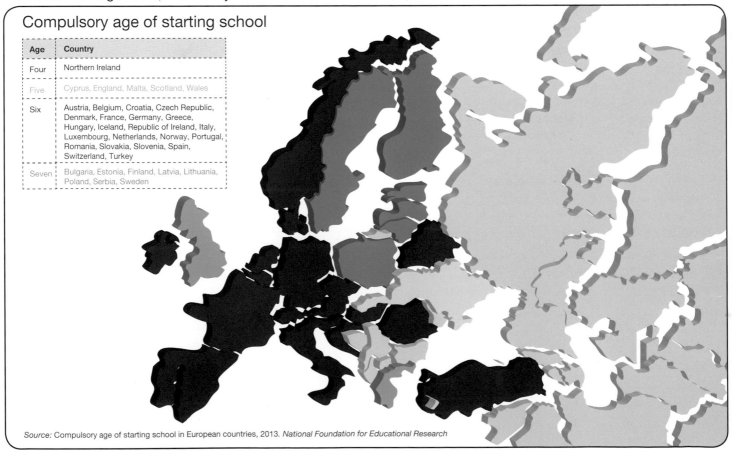

Compulsory age of starting school

Age	Country
Four	Northern Ireland
Five	Cyprus, England, Malta, Scotland, Wales
Six	Austria, Belgium, Croatia, Czech Republic, Denmark, France, Germany, Greece, Hungary, Iceland, Republic of Ireland, Italy, Luxembourg, Netherlands, Norway, Portugal, Romania, Slovakia, Slovenia, Spain, Switzerland, Turkey
Seven	Bulgaria, Estonia, Finland, Latvia, Lithuania, Poland, Serbia, Sweden

Source: Compulsory age of starting school in European countries, 2013. *National Foundation for Educational Research*

a central mechanism in learning. One book by Sergio and Vivien Pellis reviewed many other studies to show that playful activity leads to synaptic growth, particularly in the frontal cortex – the part of the brain responsible for all the uniquely human, higher mental functions.

A range of experimental psychology studies, including my own work, have consistently demonstrated the superior learning and motivation arising from playful as opposed to instructional approaches to learning in children.

There are two crucial processes which underpin this relationship. First, playful activity has been shown to support children's early development of representational skills, which is fundamental to language use. One 2006 study by US academics James Christie and Kathleen Roskos, reviewed evidence that a playful approach to language learning offers the most powerful support for the early development of phonological and literacy skills.

Second, through all kinds of physical, social and constructional play, such as building with blocks or making models with household junk, children develop their skills of intellectual and emotional 'self-regulation'. This helps them develop awareness of their own mental processes – skills that have been clearly demonstrated to be the key predictors of educational achievement and a range of other positive life outcomes.

Longer-term impacts

Within educational research, a number of longitudinal studies have provided evidence of long-term outcomes of play-based learning. A 2002 US study by Rebecca Marcon, for example, demonstrated that by the end of their sixth year in school, children whose pre-school model had been academically-directed achieved significantly lower marks in comparison to children who had attended child-initiated, play-based pre-school programmes.

A number of other studies have specifically addressed the issue

of the length of pre-school play-based experience and the age at which children begin to be formally taught the skills of literacy and numeracy. In a 2004 longitudinal study of 3,000 children funded by the Department of Education itself, Oxford's Kathy Sylva and colleagues showed that an extended period of high-quality, play-based pre-school education made a significant difference to academic learning and well-being through the primary school years. They found a particular advantage for children from disadvantaged backgrounds.

Studies in New Zealand comparing children who began formal literacy instruction at age five or age seven have shown that by the age of 11 there was no difference in reading ability level between the two groups. But the children who started at five developed less positive attitudes to reading, and showed poorer text comprehension than those children who had started later.

This evidence, directly addressing the consequences of the introduction of early formal schooling, combined with the evidence on the positive impact of extended playful experiences, raises important questions about the current direction of travel of early childhood education policy in England.

There is an equally substantial body of evidence concerning the worrying increase in stress and mental health problems among children in England and other countries where early childhood education is being increasingly formalised. It suggests there are strong links between these problems and a loss of playful experiences and increased achievement pressures. In the interests of children's educational achievements and their emotional well-being, the UK Government should take this evidence seriously.

11 July 2014

⇨ The above information is reprinted with kind permission from The Conversation. Please visit www.theconversation.com for further information.

FactCheck: when can you leave education?

'We have increased the age to which all young people in England are required to continue in education or training.'

The background

Thousands of teenagers got their GCSE results today. Many pupils will stay on to do A-levels, but some 16-year-olds will have had enough of school.

For the first time this year, the law requires school-leavers to stay on in some kind of education or training until the age of 18.

That sounds like a cast-iron rule, but in reality the Government has made things a little more flexible.

The analysis

The Government has changed the rules for school leavers, so if you started in year 11 in September last year, you will have to continue in education or training until your 18th birthday.

That covers most pupils who got their GCSE results today, and the Government says they now have to take one of three options:

⇨ Full-time study in a school, college or with a training provider.

⇨ Full-time work or volunteering combined with part-time education or training.

⇨ An apprenticeship.

This is partly an attempt to cut the country's historically high levels of young people who are NEET (not in education, employment or training).

An OECD study from 2012 found that 18 per cent of people in the UK had left school without doing A-levels, putting the country at number 25 out of 36 for drop-out rates.

NEET rates have dropped in recent months but remain worryingly high. In April to June 2014 eight per cent of people aged 16 to 18 were not in education, employment or training, the lowest second-quarter figure since records began in 2000.

The Government has raised the participation age to 18 via the Education and Skills Act 2008, which places a legal 'duty' on the pupil (not their parents) to participate in some kind of education or training.

But what does that really mean? What happens to young people who refuse? Err...nothing.

The Government's advice to parents reads: 'The law has changed, but there will be no action taken against any young people who don't participate. We want to encourage your child to participate because of the benefits it will bring.'

There was some talk from the Prime Minister about stopping young people who were NEET from getting benefits, but this won't happen until after the election.

As far as we can tell (information from the Department for Education has not been forthcoming yet) the welfare rules haven't changed, which means 16- and 17-year-olds who aren't in work or on a course can access some, though by no means all, state benefits.

Even though there are no penalties for not taking part, local councils are apparently expected to track down young people who don't play ball.

'Your local authority is responsible for identifying and supporting 16–17 year–olds who are not participating and will be working to ensure that young people are enrolled on a suitable education or training place.'

Similarly, the Government is asking employers to give young workers some kind of part-time education or training, but not making them.

DfE advice is that under-18s working fulltime should also study for 'a minimum of 280 guided learning hours per year, which is the equivalent to one day per week but doesn't necessarily have to be taken

that way – it could be distance or evening learning for example'.

Very flexible. In fact it's pretty clear that it doesn't have to be taken at all: 'There are no duties on employers in relation to RPA (Raising the Participation Age), so there will be no action taken against you if your employee fails to undertake part-time training.'

In fact, the 2008 legislation did place two duties on employers – to check that a young worker is enrolled on a suitable training course and to agree hours that will let them study – but these parts of the Act 'will not be introduced', the Government assures employers.

'We think that employers will encourage young people to train without the need for burdensome new duties and so we have decided not to commence these two duties in 2013.'

The verdict

This is a curious situation. On the face of it, the law has been changed so that 16-year-olds must stay in education or training until they are 18. But what happens if you break the law? Nothing.

Things are even more relaxed when it comes to employers making sure that their teenage staff do some kind of training as well as working.

That is apparently the intention, but the Government has decided not to implement its own legislation. So what happens to employers if young people choose not to study as well as work? Nothing.

21 August 2013

⇨ The above information is reprinted with kind permission from Channel 4 News. Please visit www.channel4.com for further information.

© *Channel 4 2015*

Could lengthening post-16 education just be delaying unemployment?

David Kingman reports on the recent warning from Ofsted that too many young people are falling 'inevitably' into 'NEET' status once they leave compulsory post-16 education.

Following changes to the law which have been implemented by the Coalition Government, young people in England now have to remain in compulsory education until the age of 17, rising to 18 from summer 2015. In theory, this should be a very good thing for them: in the modern 'knowledge economy', the more education you have the better off you are likely to be in the long term.

However, the schools inspectorate Ofsted has recently warned that for young people who are already struggling at school, keeping them there for an additional two years may simply be postponing their 'inevitable' transition towards 'NEET' status – government shorthand for young people who are Not in Employment, Education or Training. So is more schooling necessarily such a good thing?

Uncertain future

Ofsted have argued that it is 'simply not enough' to keep young people shepherded in schools and further education institutions if they are not doing anything which will lead to them eventually leaving with sufficient qualifications and experience to enjoy success in the labour market.

Ofsted have recently undertaken research which looks at how the first cohort of young people to be compelled to stay in compulsory education until the age of 17 are faring under the new arrangements. Parts of the report were highly critical of the current system, arguing that too many teenagers are receiving substandard teaching in English and maths in particular, while too many schools and colleges are not doing enough to ensure that their students progress on to decent jobs and apprenticeship or training schemes.

The schools inspectorate is particularly concerned that large numbers of young people seem to be dropping out of their courses and then effectively disappearing from local authority records because there is no efficient system for monitoring where young people who leave their courses end up. Ofsted recommended that the system for monitoring how young people are progressing with their education at all levels needs to be improved.

There are currently thought to be around 1.8 million people aged 16 to 24 who are classed as NEET, although Ofsted believes that the limitations of the current monitoring system mean this is probably an underestimate.

Lack of improvement

Ofsted's warning came at almost exactly the same time as the Government launched new statistics showing how people who stay at school to retake poor GCSE results tend to fare by the age of 18. Just over half of all students who failed to get grades A* to C in English or maths in 2011 stayed in school to try and retake them, but the figures show that only 6.5% eventually achieved this standard in English and only 7% in maths.

These findings imply that young people who are struggling at school at age 16 rarely show signs of improvement if they are remain in school for additional years of teaching. Given that it must be people in this category who would have been more likely to leave school at 16 under the old system, this worrying lack of improvement

suggests that forcing these pupils to stay in school for longer may be of only questionable benefit.

Speaking at the launch of Ofsted's report, Chief Inspector of Schools Sir Michael Wilshaw warned that England's system of post-16 education is still failing far too many young people:

'The gap between the good intentions of government policy in relation to this age group and the reality of what is happening on the ground is worryingly wide. The simple truth of what's happening at the moment is that too many of our young people, particularly those from disadvantaged backgrounds and those who want to follow vocational pathways, are not yet being well served by these programmes.'

18 September 2014

⇨ The above information is reprinted with kind permission from The Intergenerational Foundation. Please visit www. if.org.uk or www.if.org.uk/about/ schools-fact-sheets for further information.

© *The Intergenerational Foundation 2015*

Employers want education system to better prepare young people for life outside school gates – CBI/Pearson survey

Help schools develop the key skills needed for working life.

Businesses want the education system to better prepare young people with the attitudes and attributes they need to succeed in the world of work. That's according to the *Gateway to Growth: CBI/Pearson Education and Skills Survey, 2014*.

In the survey of 291 companies employing nearly 1.5 million people, over half (61%) are concerned about the resilience and self-management of school leavers and a third (33%) with their attitude to work. By contrast, nearly all firms (96%) are satisfied with young peoples' IT abilities when they enter the workplace.

Firms want primary schools to focus on developing literacy and numeracy (85%) with around one-third not satisfied with these skills among school leavers. Half (52%) are urging schools to develop a greater awareness of working life among 14–19-year-olds with support from businesses. Companies are prepared to play their part with two-thirds (66%) willing to take on a larger role in the school careers system.

John Cridland, CBI Director-General, said:

'Businesses feel very strongly that the education system must better prepare young people for life outside the school gates, or risk wasting their talents.

'The journey from school towards the world of work can be daunting, so we must support schools and teachers to help develop the skills, character and attitudes students need to progress in life.

'We're hearing the right noises from politicians of all colours, but the need for genuine reform on the ground remains.

'We need young people who are rigorous, rounded and grounded, and business stands ready to play its part.'

Rod Bristow, President of Pearson Core Markets, said:

'Everyone agrees that young people should be better supported as they prepare for the workplace – today business leaders echo the voices of teachers, Ministers and indeed young people themselves in calling for a more joined up approach to the transition from education to employment. The challenge now is to grasp the nettle so we bring employment and education opportunities together to meet the urgent social and economic need of creating a more highly-skilled workforce.

'Through our World Class Qualifications programme, Pearson is working with employers and education experts from around the world to ensure that young people in the UK are equipped with the skills they will need to prosper in education or in the workplace.'

Key findings include:

⇨ Too many young people leave education not equipped with enough knowledge of their chosen job/career (school leavers 56%, graduates 30%)

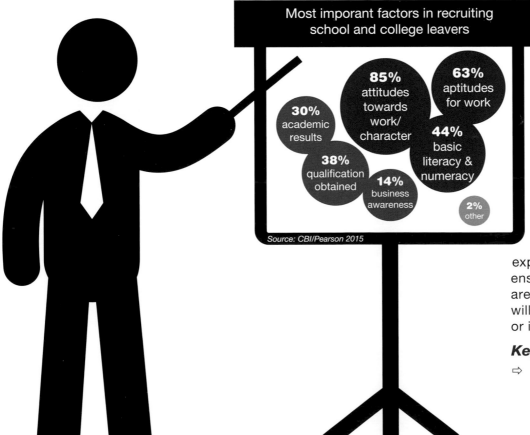

Most imporant factors in recruiting school and college leavers

- 30% academic results
- 85% attitudes towards work/character
- 63% aptitudes for work
- 38% qualification obtained
- 44% basic literacy & numeracy
- 14% business awareness
- 2% other

Source: CBI/Pearson 2015

or relevant work experience (school leavers 55%, graduates 37%). This reflects concerns that careers advice is simply not good enough to help young people make informed choices (80%).

⇨ Businesses recognise the need to support schools with 80% forging links of some type with at least one school or college.

⇨ The skills gap is getting worse – 58% of firms are not confident they will have sufficient highly skilled staff available for their needs in the future. A quarter (28%) of firms who need technicians qualified in science, technology, engineering or maths already report difficulty recruiting and a third (35%) anticipate problems in the next three years.

⇨ Nearly half of employers (44%) have organised training to tackle weaknesses in basic numeracy, literacy and IT for adult employees and more than a quarter (28%) for those who have joined directly from school or college.

The CBI is urging reform of Ofsted so that academic progress and the development of character are both prioritised in schools. It argues of the need to clearly set out what we want our schools to deliver and effectively hold them to account against this.

Such changes can help build support for a more tailored curriculum between 14 and 18, based around individual learning plans.

The UK's leading business organisation has challenged the automatic assumption that an academic path is the best route to success for young people, calling for the delivery of gold-standard vocational 'A levels' as a viable and rewarding alternative. It also wants the requirement for work experience at key stage 4 restored and for more business engagement with schools.

On the growing skills gap and education reform, John Cridland added:

'There is a crisis in UK skills right now and our incapacity to meet growing demands for higher skills is putting the long-term prospects of the UK economy at risk. We need to create more apprenticeships, but also retrain current workers with in-demand skills in key sectors.

'We need a system that better reflects how well a school's culture nurtures the behaviours and attitudes young people will need. Success should be measured by where young people go once they have left school or college, not on exam results alone. A switch by Ofsted inspectors to the kind of broad-based quality assurance that has served British business so well over the past 20 years is critical to this.'

Other findings include:

Science, technology, engineering and maths (STEM) skills in short supply

The recovery faces mounting risk of skill shortages

More than half of employers are aware of weaknesses in the core competencies of at least some of their employees in literacy (54%), numeracy (53%) and IT skills (61%). But most employers consider overall skill levels among their employees as satisfactory with more than two thirds (69%) rating the skills of their high-skilled employees as good.

Science, technology, engineering and maths (STEM) skills in short supply

Businesses have concerns about both the quality (48%) and quantity (46%) of STEM graduates, and report that too many lack general workplace experience (39%).

Businesses are stepping up skills investment

Far more firms plan to increase their investment in employee training and development during the coming year than plan to cut back (producing a positive balance of +26%).

Shaping a fully effective apprenticeship system

Two thirds of those offering apprenticeships (69%) plan to extend their programmes in future while across all respondents one in eight (13%) plans to start offering apprenticeships in the next three years.

Raising the performance of our schools

The most important factors employers weigh up when recruiting school and college leavers are their attitudes to work (85%), their general aptitudes (63%), and literacy and numeracy (44%). These rank well ahead of formal academic results (30%).

Businesses recognise the need to support schools

Among employers with links to schools and colleges, the most common forms of support are offering work experience placements (77%) and providing careers advice and talks (67%).

Careers advice: not yet fit for purpose

Short-term work placements of a week or two are by far the most common type of work experience offered by businesses (89%), but almost half (46%) also offer longer-term paid internships.

Developing the right skills in graduates

A degree in a STEM subject gives graduates a clear advantage in the jobs market, with nearly half of employers (48%) reporting that they prefer graduates with these qualifications.

Businesses and universities: partnering for growth

More than two thirds (70%) of businesses have developed links of some type with universities and nearly half of firms (48%) are looking to grow their ties with universities in the future.

4 July 2014

⇨ The above information is reprinted with kind permission from CBI. Please visit www.cbi.org.uk for further information.

Higher Apprenticeships better for jobs than university degrees say public

Significant public support for degree-level apprenticeships as an alternative to traditional university degrees is revealed in new polling, presented to delegates at an international summit on apprenticeships and vocational education organised by the Sutton Trust in partnership with Pearson.

One third (34%) of people say a degree-level apprenticeship would be better for somebody's future career prospects than a university degree, while two in ten (21%) think a traditional degree would be better. The new poll of 1,728 adults aged 16–25 in England by Ipsos MORI showed that a further third of people (33%) feel both are equally valuable.

The summit will be opened this morning by the Leader of the Opposition, Rt Hon Ed Miliband MP and will be addressed by the Minister of State for Skills and Enterprise, Matthew Hancock MP.

Other polling to be presented to delegates attending the Higher Ambitions summit in London shows that:

⇨ More than half of young people (55%) aged 11–16 say they would be interested in an apprenticeship rather than going to university if it was available in a job they wanted to do, but only 30% say that their teachers have ever discussed the idea of apprenticeships with them at school. (Ipsos MORI, 11–16-year-olds)

⇨ Qualitative research carried out amongst 14-16-year-olds found that they reported very few conversations about post-16 options with teachers, who they felt were more concerned with current qualifications. (Britain Thinks)

⇨ Only 26% of teachers think (to a great or some extent) there are enough apprenticeships at A-level standard or higher available. 65% said they would rarely or never advise a high-achieving student

to consider an apprenticeship. (NFER Teacher Omnibus)

The Ipsos-MORI polling of adults aged 16–75 also shows that:

⇨ Two thirds of the public believe that most apprenticeships should be designed to meet A-level standard (Level 3) or higher, whereas government data shows that two thirds of apprenticeships started by young people in 2012/13 were only at GCSE standard (Level 2).

⇨ 56% of parents say they are likely to encourage their children to go for a degree, while only 40% would encourage them to do an apprenticeship.

The summit follows last year's Boston Consulting Group report for the Sutton Trust which called for an extra 150–300,000 apprenticeships at A-level standard (Level 3) or higher and on last Friday's Pearson/CBI skills survey which showed serious concerns among employers about recruiting apprentices, graduates and technicians particularly in scientific or engineering roles.

Official figures highlighted in the delegates' report show that in 2012/13, there were 180,000 apprenticeship starts for 16–24-year-olds to GCSE standard (intermediate), 97,000 to A-level standard (advanced) and 3,000 degree-level (Higher) apprenticeships.

The average apprenticeship for 16–18-year-olds lasted 17 months but for 19–24-year-olds it was shorter, at 14 months. Around a third of young people's apprenticeships lasted a year or less.

Conor Ryan, Director of Research at the Sutton Trust, said: 'There is a growing appetite for real apprenticeships among young people and the wider public. But there are still not nearly enough apprenticeships at A-level or degree standard available. It is vital that this gap is addressed.'

'Our research has shown that in other European countries, particularly in Germany and Switzerland, three-year good quality apprenticeships are a serious option for all young people. Despite some recent improvements, we still have a mountain to climb to match ambitions in England.'

Rod Bristow, President of Pearson Core Markets, said: 'Vocational education's time has come: we know that young people want it and employers need it. The UK has the opportunity to put high quality vocational education and apprenticeships at the heart of our education system and our plan for economic growth.

'We know that the best vocational systems around the world combine the academic skills of "know-what" and "know why" with the more applied skills of "know-how". All jobs in the 21st century value not just what people know, but what they can do. In the UK many vocational students are already making progress onto HE or into great jobs, but if we are to compete with the best we need to be more focused, more aspirational, more relevant.

'Pearson is working with employers and international education experts through our World Class Qualifications programme to ensure that young people in the UK gain the blend of skills that will allow them to flourish in education and employment.'

Other speakers at today's summit include Andreas Schleicher, Director of Education and Skills at the OECD, Professor Alison Wolf, Graham Stuart MP, chairman of the Education Select Committee, Professor Michael Barber and Ben Page, chief executive of Ipsos-Mori.

8 July 2014

⇨ The above information is reprinted with kind permission from the Sutton Trust. Please visit www.suttontrust.com for further information.

© Sutton Trust 2015

NUS launches roadmap for free education

NUS has launched its proposals on how to provide public funding for higher education.

The report, a roadmap for free education, outlines the routes that could be taken to start the debate on this issue and help politicians and vice chancellors make the right decisions on higher education reform.

The report argues that higher education could be funded by collective public investment through progressive taxation, with an increase on tax of the richest in society.

NUS is also serious about increasing business investment in higher education and believes that a modest increase in revenue from businesses channelled into higher education could remove the cost burden from students, the Government and the taxpayer.

NUS has continuously warned that forcing debt onto students as a way of funding universities was a failed experiment, and public trust in higher education funding now urgently needs to be rebuilt. In the run up to the general election, NUS is asking the Government to phase out tuition fees and restore public funding to universities as part of its manifesto.

The Government's own estimates indicate the size of outstanding student debt will increase to more than £330 billion by 2044.

The proportion of graduates failing to pay back student loans is increasing at such a rate that the Treasury is approaching the point at which it will get zero financial reward from the Government's policy of tripling tuition fees to £9,000 a year.

The threshold at which experts calculate that the Government will lose more money than it would have saved by keeping the old £3,000 tuition fee system is 48.6 per cent. Official forecasts suggested that the write-off costs for student loans had reached 45 per cent of the £10 billion in student loans made each year.

Megan Dunn, NUS Vice-President (Higher Education), said:

'Not only is a publicly funded education system achievable, it's also necessary in the current economic and political climate. Our roadmap seriously challenges those who want to bury their heads in the sand and pretend that the current broken system can be fixed with tweaks and tinkering. The clear fact is that the current system we have is completely unsustainable.

'The Government's own figures show that the prospect of a huge black hole looming over the budget is very real. It's time the Government started taking this issue seriously and committed to a new deal for students.

'We are told that we can't tax the rich because they are the "wealth creators" but we know that the real wealth creators of our society are the teachers and lecturers who are building up the knowledge and the skills of our country. We should be investing in them rather than protecting those who have driven the economy to its knees.

'Forcing debt onto students as a way of funding universities is an experiment that has failed not just students, but our country. Politicians need to recognise that we will only achieve a sustainable higher education funding system if we abandon the discredited regime of sky-high fees and debts altogether.'

17 November 2014

⇨ The above information is reprinted with kind permission from NUS. Please visit www.nus.org.uk for further information.

A roadmap for free education

Extract from the Foreword by Toni Pearce, NUS President and Megan Dunn, NUS Vice-President (Higher Education).

At the peak of the industrial revolution, we had the political ambition and the economic sense to make access to primary education universal.

70 years on, we made a similar leap forward during World War II, when it was understood that free, universal secondary education was needed to rebuild and strengthen the country.

It's been another 70 years since the 1944 Education Act, and it is time for another leap forward. The time is right for free, universal tertiary education.

A commitment to free, publicly-funded higher education is a commitment to ensuring that our universities are seen for what they really are – invaluable national assets – and remain as such. The 21st century demands that tertiary education is treated with the same degree of public importance as primary and secondary schooling, and the National Health Service.

We need to return to the principles of public value, collaboration, and democratic accountability; and the way to do that is to return higher education to the people, to fund it through progressive taxation, and remove the destructive market forces that threaten its future.

It is time for a serious review of how tertiary education is funded and provided. We cannot expect to build a more diverse and innovative economy, and a stronger and fairer society, without radically changing the way we educate and train.

In 2084, 70 years from now, the great grandchildren of today's young people will look back on the decisions we make and either thank us for our courage in giving free education to the people, or forever condemn us for allowing the tragedy of fees, loans and debt to continue.

Government pledges to reduce teacher workload

The Deputy Prime Minister and Education Secretary outline plans as the results of the Workload Challenge survey are published.

A series of decisive measures designed to help tackle the root causes of unnecessary teacher workload have been announced today (6 February 2015) by Deputy Prime Minister Nick Clegg and Education Secretary Nicky Morgan.

A key part of the Government's plan for education is ensuring teachers can focus on what they do best – teaching and raising standards – so they can prepare young people for life in modern Britain, and not be bogged down with unnecessary tasks.

As part of this plan, thousands of teachers shared their experiences, ideas and solutions on reducing unnecessary workload by taking part in the Workload Challenge survey – the biggest Department for Education (DfE) consultation of its kind in a decade.

The survey generated more than 44,000 returns. The same themes were raised again and again by the profession as the key drivers of unnecessary and unproductive workload, including Ofsted and the pressure it places on school leaders (whether real or perceived), and from government – as well as hours spent recording data, marking and lesson-planning.

Today, Nick Clegg and Nicky Morgan responded to these calls and underlined their pledge to work with the profession to help tackle this issue by outlining a number of commitments, including:

⇨ commitments by Ofsted:

- not to change their handbook or framework during the school year, except when absolutely necessary

- to keep updating their new myths and facts document stating what inspectors do and do not expect to see

- from 2016 onwards, to look to make the handbook shorter and simpler, so that schools can more easily understand how inspectors will reach their judgements

⇨ giving schools more notice of significant changes to the curriculum, exams and accountability, and not making changes to qualifications in the academic year or during a course, unless there are urgent reasons for doing so

⇨ making it easier for teachers to find examples of what works in other schools, and research about the best way to do things like marking, data management and planning by bringing together a central repository of evidence

⇨ support for headteachers to carry out their demanding jobs by reviewing all leadership training, including reviewing the opportunities available for coaching and mentoring for leaders

⇨ tracking teacher workload over the coming years by carrying out a large scale, robust survey in early spring 2016, and every two years from then

Deputy Prime Minister Nick Clegg said:

'Every school is only as good as the teachers that work there, and I know that some have been left feeling browbeaten and under-valued, engaged in a constant battle with bureaucracy.

'These are the people that work day in, day out, doing a fantastic job in helping shape our children's futures. Yet thousands have told us that they're simply not able to focus on the job at hand because of the burdensome workloads they're faced with. It's about time we changed that.

'That's why we've listened and we're making changes now to help ease that burden and allow teachers to spend more time doing the job they signed up for in the first place. This is just the start, but it's an important first step in helping build a better education system and fairer society which puts pupils at its heart so they all have a chance to succeed.'

Secretary of State for Education Nicky Morgan said:

'We had an absolutely fantastic response to the Workload Challenge and I'd like to thank everyone who took time out of their busy days to contribute.

'It is no secret that we have made some very important changes in schools – changes that we know have increased the pressure on many teachers. All of these changes were vital, though, and I'm pleased to say that standards are now higher and a million more children are in good or outstanding schools.

'Now we want to support the profession to tackle the issue of unnecessary and unproductive workload, which I know many teachers are concerned about and that is stopping them from giving time to what really matters – inspiring young people to achieve their potential.

'The ideas we have received helped to build a picture of the root causes of unnecessary workload.

'We know there is no quick fix but we hope the commitments we have outlined today will support and empower the profession and free up teachers to focus on what matters most in their jobs.'

Sir Andrew Carter said:

'I'm very pleased to see the Government's response to the Workload Challenge consultation, and I am particularly pleased to see the proposals for reviewing the support for headteachers and drawing together evidence for teachers.

'The actions set out here are the right ones – it is now important for everyone in education to work together to ensure an effective work-life balance is achievable for all. We know that many leaders are already managing this in schools and it is vital we continue to share effective approaches throughout the system.'

Chief Inspector of Schools Sir Michael Wilshaw said:

'I welcome the focus of this report on reducing work that does not directly contribute to raising standards for pupils.

'We have worked closely with school leaders and the Department for Education to confirm the facts about what Ofsted expects to see in schools. In particular, our clarification document has been well received by teachers and is helping to dispel some of the myths that may have led to unnecessary workloads.

'This week, we confirmed a number of radical changes to education inspection, which will see frequent but shorter inspections of good schools and further education and skills providers. These changes take effect in September and will place a greater emphasis on professional dialogue between headteachers and inspectors. They will help school leaders to concentrate on the things that matter the most – making sure there is good teaching, robust assessment and a positive and respectful learning culture in schools.

'It is very important that schools maintain a sense of proportion when preparing for an Ofsted inspection. If they are devoting their energies to getting things right for pupils, then an Ofsted inspection will take care of itself.'

The pledges outlined today come on top of the action already taken by the Government to reduce unnecessary workload for teachers and support the profession, including:

⇨ Ofsted's myth-buster – a simple set of statements to help schools dispel myths about inspections, which can lead to schools providing reams of additional paperwork for inspectors

⇨ cutting more than 21,000 pages of guidance, streamlining the inspection process and making it clear that formal written plans are not expected for every lesson

⇨ supporting the creation of a new, independent, professional body for teaching – a college of teaching – that will give the profession greater responsibility over things like professional standards and development, placing teaching on an equal footing with high-status professions like law and medicine

⇨ establishing a new fund to support more high-quality, evidence-based professional development programmes – the kind of professional development opportunities that teachers and school leaders have long argued for

⇨ publishing new, high-quality headteacher standards, providing them with aspirational standards of excellence that will support them to get the best out of their staff and pupils.

6 February 2015

⇨ The above information is reprinted with kind permission from the Department for Education. Please visit www.gov.uk for further information.

What does data tell us about how to tackle heavy teacher workloads?

The Guardian *looks at the figures behind the Government's workload survey and call for your views on how we can free teachers from bureaucracy.*

By Sarah Marsh

In October last year, the Deputy Prime Minister, Nick Clegg, pledged to tackle excessive teacher workloads. He vowed to stop the runaway train of bureaucracy in its tracks, 'giving our teachers more time to do what they do best'.

Four months later, after 44,000 teachers responded to the consultation, the Government released their plan of action. They promised no more major policy changes during the academic year and announced that Ofsted would need to give more clarification on what they are looking for – among other moves.

Their suggestions have, however, come under fire. Mary Bousted, general secretary of the Association of Teachers and Lecturers (ATL), said: 'Teachers will feel ignored and bitterly disappointed that the Government is doing nothing tangible to cut their workload.'

So, we decided to take a closer look at the data behind the survey. We've put together some graphs on the main areas that teachers highlighted as an issue. Take a look at the information below and tell us your ideas on a plan of action to effectively free teachers from bureaucracy.

The five main areas putting teachers under pressure

1. Ofsted

The table below shows that trusting teachers and tackling Ofsted was high on a list of ways to reduce workloads.

Suggested solutions to workload issues

Suggested solution	Percentage
Modify marking arrangements	32%
Reduce need to input data	25%
Increase PPA time	25%
Trust teachers as professionals	24%
Reduce frequency of curriculum/exam changes	22%
Review/change Ofsted	21%
Delegate admin duties	19%
Modify marking arrangements	18%

Source: Department for Education, 2015

In fact, a lot of the factors contributing to workload outlined in the Government's consultation – for example, data and marking – are driven in some way by our high-stakes accountability system.

It's worth noting that high performance doesn't necessarily follow high-stakes accountability. We know international tables, namely Pisa, aren't the be-all-and-end-all of education, but they're a firm favourite of politicians. So it's interesting to note that Finland, lauded for their education performance, stopped inspecting schools in the 1990s.

In their response, the Government focused on clarifying what Ofsted expect from schools and taking a closer look at their quality control. The inspectorate will be clear about what is and is not required, review how reports are written and introduce shorter inspection for good schools from September 2015 – among other reforms.

2. Marking

Marking was one of the biggest issues for teachers, according to the consultation;

32% of respondents said that modifying marking arrangements would be a good way to make a real difference to their workloads.

As shown in the chart below, 63% of teachers said the excessive level of detail required made tasks harder. When commenting on the findings, Bousted said that every piece of work does not require deep marking but, rather, the level of time spent should be appropriate to the work undertaken by the student. If a teacher is looking, for example, at a draft essay they should mark less thoroughly than they would a final piece. Bousted also suggested that verbal feedback could be given in some circumstances.

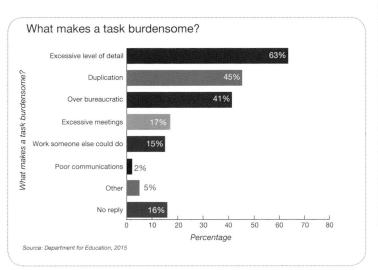

What makes a task burdensome?

Source: Department for Education, 2015

3. Data

Recording and inputting data was one of the most commonly cited 'unnecessary' task teachers found themselves doing.

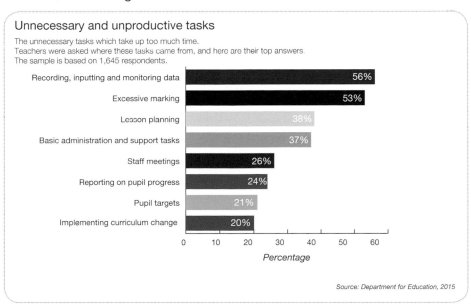

Unnecessary and unproductive tasks

The unnecessary tasks which take up too much time.
Teachers were asked where these tasks came from, and here are their top answers.
The sample is based on 1,645 respondents.

Source: Department for Education, 2015

A big issue with data is duplication; teachers find themselves recording the same information in different ways for different purposes.

The Government proposed setting up a data management panel to work with teachers and others to come up with principles for data management best practice.

This is a welcome move – any help with working out what reams of data can be ignored or improved upon, surely shouldn't be shunned.

4. A lack of PPA time

A substantial 25% of teachers called for more of planning, preparation and assessment time in the research.

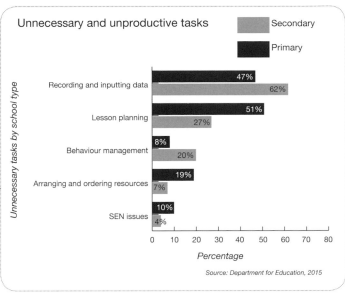

Source: Department for Education, 2015

It's also interesting that the majority (51%) of respondents from primary schools – in comparison to 27% in secondary schools – found the workload for weekly lesson planning a burden. It's worth considering whether primary teachers need a better way to share lesson ideas, or more planning time.

5. Meetings

Lots of teachers (17%) included an excessive number of meetings as one of the unnecessary tasks taking up too much time in their day. A lot of the meetings were not always relevant to them and their content duplicated information already distributed.

Could there be a cap on the number of meetings per week? With the advent of email, information is now easy to circulate, but how can you ensure teachers are properly supported in implementing new strategies? And is it important for teachers to have face-to-face time in a very people-facing job?

12 February 2015

⇨ The above information is reprinted with kind permission from *The Guardian*. Please visit www. theguardian.com for further information.

A teacher speaks out: 'I'm effectively being forced out of a career that I wanted to love'

When Sam Burton began teaching three years ago, he was determined to thrive. But after spells at an academy and a special educational needs school, he's had enough. Here, he tells the story of how even an energetic young teacher can struggle with the demands of modern teaching.

Being a good teacher means uncovering themes which will engage kids, trawling websites and libraries for films and texts as stimuli. It entails writing four different intentionally-flawed versions of a suspenseful story for them to modify in their first lesson, and five different tiers of riddles about 3D shapes for them to tackle in the second, all before 8am.

It means using outdated software to create worksheets with seven different cartoon characters to motivate students with severe learning difficulties, and spending break times enlarging these for students with visual impairments.

It means composing science songs to the tune of The Gap Band's 'Oops Upside Your Head'

at nine in the evening. It requires giving each student feedback every day, verbally and in writing, in each subject. It necessitates arranging and booking trips, often at lunchtime. It needs people to deliver lessons with enthusiasm and energy and flexibility all day, and to call upon reserves of patience if students are challenging.

In some of the classrooms I have taught in, this might range from students being rude, to hitting, scratching and biting on a daily basis.

Fortunately, I am excellent at doing all of the above and even enjoy it, though it leaves me physically drained and marinating in cortisol come 4pm.

Regrettably, it's not so simple. At the end of the school day, I should be checking how students did that day, giving them feedback and preparing the next day's lessons. This is why I entered teaching – to get young people to enjoy learning. This alone would ensure I stay in the building until past 6pm, which would be taxing but OK. Yet there is a range of other duties that I can be reprimanded for not fulfilling, which I then end up doing instead of preparing lessons.

I am expected to input assessment data into spreadsheets and copy it into other programs click by click, working out manually whether a percentage equates to a 'P6c' or a 'P6b'. (Data which might have been massaged by successive teachers pressured into 'generous' assessment.) I assess work that has already been assessed by completing lavish 'Next Step' stickers to satisfy Ofsted (this is in a special educational needs school where students cannot read).

I complete incident reports, carry out teaching assistant appraisals, produce three types of reports when one would do, file students' work, produce reports on attendance, and monitor a subject area to ensure others' planning and teaching is high quality. Some of these tasks are necessary, while some represent repetitive, inefficient paper chasing for the eyes of inspectors. Anyway, the point is I can't do all of them.

The current teaching culture – at least where I've worked – is that it's normal to work evenings and weekends, despite starting at 7.30am. Not the easing-yourself-

into-work-over-your-emails sort of 7.30am start – it's the 'If I haven't got resources ready for six different lessons by 8.45am, I'm going to have a terrible day and possibly get in trouble for having a terrible day' sort.

This is compounded by utter frustration that the reason I'm scrabbling around frantically when it's still dark outside, and exhausted and stressed during lessons, is that I was prevented from doing the basics of my job by the aforementioned administrative burden.

'I am expected to input assessment data into spreadsheets and copy it into other programs click by click, working out manually whether a percentage equates to a "P6c" or a "P6b". (Data which might have been massaged by successive teachers pressured into "generous" assessment)'

The workload is un-audited. New duties are not assessed for the effect they will have on existing workload. There is an implicit (and offensive, frankly) assumption that I am not already working to capacity – that when a new format for reports is introduced which will require an extra 15 hours of work over a two-week period, that I have 15 more hours spare. I have discussed the impact this has on teaching with my managers and been told simply that it is not allowed to have an impact; teaching standards are non-negotiable regardless of workload. It was explained to me that, 'You can't assume I know what your workload is like' by a senior teacher.

I work 50 to 60 hours a week, yet am judged three times per year in classroom observations which make or break me regardless of the everyday success of my work. Teachers are so petrified of the consequences of having a bad observation that it is common practice to repeat a successful lesson from the previous week. I cannot reconcile myself with letting my students down like this in order to temporarily preserve my career for another three months. As for protection, the culture of fear is endemic: as a newly qualified teacher, it was suggested to me that if I joined a union someone could find a reason to put me on capability procedure.

The fear seems to permeate from above: I've had three head teachers and the thing they've had in common is an inability to change things, as their hands are tied by the same external demands for accountability and good data.

Some didn't hesitate to email late at night or at weekends to say that pencils should not be less than 8cm long. Others made it clear that they didn't want teachers taking work home or coming in at the weekend, but could do nothing to reduce a workload which made doing that a prerequisite of the job. During Ofsted inspections, I have fainted at my desk having worked 42 hours in two and a half days, slept on a colleague's sofa and worn his underwear for two days.

There is a suspicious sense that young teachers are taken advantage of: we are grateful to have a job, and less likely to know or assert our rights. We have fewer family commitments and are generally more physically robust. (I have been told by older teachers who have taught my class that they 'couldn't' teach them for more than one day because it was too exhausting.)

Under the current Government and through my training route, Teach First, there has been an increased sense of prestige accompanying teaching as a graduate career, previously only associated with corporate grad schemes. Also seemingly borrowed from the corporate sector, however, is a perverse sense that 'resilience' and a work ethic are the most desirable qualities in new teachers, over empathy, flexible thought, and even being properly qualified, as if a job being punishing is what makes it worth doing.

'The only way to do a good job is to work breathless 12-plus-hour days every day, which I cannot keep up. I am not content, however, to work less and do a bad job for the children. I am angry that I am effectively being forced out of a career that I wanted to love'

I've done better than some and have managed three years. But I haven't finished reading more than five books in that time. The habit has been trampled out of me by paperwork and exhaustion. Is that someone you would want teaching your children?

I am a young, energetic person with a first-class degree from a top university. I have been graded an 'outstanding' teacher by colleagues; I like working hard. Really. My grievance has little to do with pay and pensions – for most young teachers, remaining in the profession until pensionable age is a ludicrous prospect, due to unsustainable workload. The only way to do a good job is to work breathless 12-plus-hour days every day, which I cannot keep up. I am not content, however, to work less and do a bad job for the children. I am angry that I am effectively being forced out of a career that I wanted to love.

But at least I wrote all that without mentioning Michael Gove.

30 August 2014

⇨ The above information is reprinted with kind permission from *The Independent*. Please visit www.independent.co.uk for further information.

At what cost? Exposing the impact of poverty on school life

Executive summary from the report supported by The Children's Society.

Poverty affects every area of a child's life, and this is no different for school. We may believe that the UK offers a free education, but what children wear at school, what they eat, whether they can join in with friends, even which classes they choose to attend, are all affected by their ability to afford the costs of school.

'Well I know that mum has a lot that she has to do to keep us inschool and it's quite a struggle'

Young person

The inquiry heard how poverty can make children feel singled out, stigmatised and bullied. It affects whether they are properly fed and clothed, and in turn their ability to concentrate and engage in learning.

Too many children are missing out on the opportunity to make the very most of their education, because they struggle to afford the costs of school life.

A lot needs to change in order to ensure that children can afford the costs of the school day, and the recommendations in this report represent an action plan which would take a big step towards addressing this.

An overview of the cost of school

'…that is part of the effect of child poverty, exclusion'

For many families, the idea of a free education is very far from reality. School-related costs make up a large portion of family budgets and parents told us that, on average, they spend £800 a year on school costs.

More than two-thirds (70%) of parents say they have struggled with the cost of school. This rises to 95% of parents who live in families that are 'not well off at all'.

At the same time, more than half (52%) of parents said they had cut back on either clothing, food or heating to afford the cost of school. Nearly half (47%) cut back on clothing, 28% on food and 29% on heating.

A quarter (25%) of parents (and more than half of those in families which were 'not well off at all') said they had borrowed money in order to afford the cost of school.

The impact on children

'There is someone in my school who lives in a block of flats and isn't really as well off and [other children] talk about her…I think she finds it really hard'

Children are acutely aware that their parents struggle with the cost of school. Where children were struggling with school costs, in many cases this led to embarrassment and bullying. Nearly two-thirds (63%) of children in families who are 'not well off at all' said they had been embarrassed because they couldn't afford an expense of school. More than a quarter (27%) said they had been bullied as a result.

More than half of children have avoided asking their parents or guardian for something school related because they thought they would struggle to afford it.

School uniform

'…if there is going to be school uniforms the school should pay for them.'

Children told the inquiry that not being able to afford the right uniform, or having a uniform that is worn out, can make children stand out.

'More than two-thirds (70%) of parents say they have struggled with the cost of school. This rises to 95% of parents who live in families that are "not well off at all"'

Guidance published by the Government tells schools that value for money for parents should be a key

priority when they set their uniform policy. Yet many schools insist on a school uniform policy which requires parents to buy expensive items of clothing emblazoned with embroidered names or logos.

More than two-thirds (71%) of parents said they had to buy either some or all items of school uniform from a specific supplier.

Parents said they spend on average £108 on school clothing for primary school children and £126 for secondary school children. But only one in five (22%) of families who are 'not well-off at all' had received any help to purchase a school uniform.

School meals

'When my mum's got the money then we can get snacks. It's 25 pence per item. We don't get snacks if it's a bad week. Sometimes we're hungry.'

School meals have an important role in this, by ensuring that children receive a healthy, nutritious meal at least once a day. This has a significant impact upon concentration, behaviour and children's ability to learn.

However, more than half of parents (52%) said they had struggled with the cost of school meals, and one in five children (20%) said they have missed out on a school meal because they didn't have enough money.

'You can always tell when someone is having free school meals, because they hold up a card and have their card inspected'

Some schools continue to deliver free school meals in a way that singles out children in poverty, leading to stigma and embarrassment. One in five children (19%) in a family that is 'not well of at all' said they had been embarrassed because their family cannot afford meals.

Materials and participation

'We get stacks of homework and most of it is on the computer... I had to tell the teacher to print out a sheet so I could just fill it in but the teacher kept saying it wasn't high enough quality homework. I would only score a five or three out of ten.'

The law states that schools cannot charge for any materials related to the delivery of the national curriculum, but it is clear many children are finding themselves expected to pay for key materials, restricting children's ability to participate fully in education. And children are avoiding certain subjects due to the additional cost of equipment or trips.

Computers and an Internet connection at home are increasingly necessary for children to complete their homework. Three in ten children whose family is 'not well off at all' said they had fallen behind at school because their family could not afford the necessary computer or Internet facilities at home.

A third of children who said their family is 'not well off at all' have fallen behind in class because their family could not afford the necessary books or materials.

'There was a history trip to the Big Pit in Wales, I didn't go on that. It was too expensive to go, Mum couldn't afford it at the time, it was 20-something pound. I come home and talked to Mum about it and we couldn't afford it... It felt bad when everyone come back and said how much an amazing time they had.'

The cost of school trips also causes problems for many children. Two in five children who live in families that are 'not well off at all' have missed a term-time school trip because of the cost.

October 2014

⇨ The above information is reprinted with kind permission from The Children's Society. Please visit www.childrenssociety.org.uk for further information.

© *The Children's Society, October 2014*

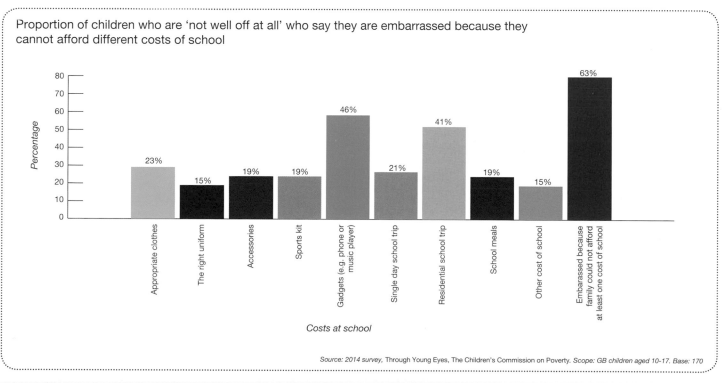

Proportion of children who are 'not well off at all' who say they are embarrassed because they cannot afford different costs of school

Costs at school

Source: 2014 survey, Through Young Eyes, The Children's Commission on Poverty. Scope: GB children aged 10-17. Base: 170

Streaming six-year-olds by ability only benefits the brightest

An article from The Conversation.

By Susan Hallam (Professor of Education and Music Psychology at UCL Institute of Education) and Samantha Parsons (Research officer, Department of Quantitative Social Science at UCL Institute of Education)

The streaming of children at primary school by their ability is actually widening the achievement gap between low and high-attaining pupils. Our research has shown that streaming in primary school leads to higher marks for children in the top class, but lower marks for those in the middle and lower classes compared to those in mixed ability classes.

Streaming – when children are placed in a class based on general ability and taught in that class for the whole time – is on the increase among five- to seven-year-olds in UK primary schools. While around 2–3% of Year 2 pupils were streamed in the 1990s, by 2007 this had increased to 17% in England, 16% in Scotland, 20% in Wales and 11% in Northern Ireland.

Streaming for six-year-olds

Our research, presented at the British Educational Research Association conference, used data from the Millennium Cohort Study (MCS) to investigate how grouping children by their ability into upper, middle and lower streams in Year 2 (six- to seven-years-old) relates to their academic progress. We also took into account other key child, family and school characteristics.

The MCS follows the lives of around 19,000 children born in the UK in 2000 to 2001. Five surveys of cohort members have been carried out so far – at nine months, three, five, seven and 11 years.

Our research focused on children in families in England where information on streaming had been provided by their primary school teacher – and we had data from the National Pupil Database on their test results at Key Stage 1 (five- to seven-years-old). The analysis was based on 2,544 children in 307 primary schools, of whom 83% (2,098) were not streamed, 8% (222) were in the 'top' stream, 5% (130) were in the 'middle' stream and 4% (94) were in the 'bottom' stream.

Top streams do better

Findings demonstrate that seven-year-olds placed in the top stream have the highest scores. Those in the middle or bottom streams are doing less well overall, and in reading in particular.

Mitigating factors

From here we took account of a wide range of child, family and school characteristics. We assessed whether this association with scores in key stage 1 was largely due to, for example, the child's earlier academic ability, their gender, how educated their parents were or the school intake.

Children's characteristics, such as their previous school performance, gender, age and health, had the greatest impact on mitigating the association between streaming and academic performance.

We found that regardless of the child's characteristics, in comparison to the majority of children taught in mixed ability classes, those in the top stream were likely to have better overall marks, while those in the middle or bottom streams were likely to have lower average marks.

Neither socio-economic factors such as parental education, income and health, nor other factors such as a child's enjoyment of school and friendships had little impact on the relationship between their stream placement and key stage 1 results.

This meant that when all child, family and school characteristics were included in the analysis, the relationship between a child's stream and his or her scores remained very significant. Compared to the majority of children in mixed ability classes, those in the top stream had higher average scores and children in the middle or bottom stream had lower average scores. The relationship only lost its statistical significance for maths scores for children in the middle stream.

Family time helps

A child's earlier academic performance was the most significant positive predictor of higher scores at age seven, whereas behaviour difficulties had the opposite effect. Being born in the autumn (meaning the child was older for their year), was also associated with greater academic progress in maths and overall performance at key stage 1.

Joint family activities were associated with higher scores across the subjects, as was how much interest parents showed in their child's education.

In many ways the findings are counter-intuitive, given that matching work to pupils' current level of attainment should enhance learning. The most likely explanation as to why this is not the case is that grouping children by ability changes teachers' expectations.

This impacts on what is taught to different groups, how it is taught and the unspoken messages given to pupils. Schools need to be aware of these issues when making decisions about structured ability grouping.

25 September 2014

Do academies make use of their autonomy?

Research report.

By Rob Crin, Department for Education

1. Headline findings

A representative online survey of 720 academies which were open on 1 May 2013 examined their uses of autonomy available to them to decide how best to run their schools. The headline findings were:

Academies have used their freedoms to innovate and improve

➪ 79 per cent have changed or plan to change their curriculum

➪ 90 per cent have procured or planned to procure services previously provided by the LA

➪ 84 per cent are now linking pay to performance

This is helping them raise standards for their pupils

➪ Two thirds believe these changes have improved attainment

➪ The most important changes were seen to be those to the curriculum and leadership

It is also helping them to raise standards for pupils in other schools via collaboration

➪ 87 per cent of academies support other schools (72 per cent support schools they did not support before becoming academies)

➪ 96 per cent of outstanding academies support other schools

2. Summary of main findings

Reasons for conversion

➪ There was no dominant main reason for conversion but the most frequently cited were: to raise educational standards; to obtain more funding for front-line education; and to gain greater freedom to use funding as you see fit.

➪ Schools which converted to academy status shortly after May 2010 were more likely to do so for financial gain. More recent converters are more likely to do so for opportunities for collaboration.

➪ Those in Multi-Academy Trusts (MATs) and primary schools were more likely than standalone academies and secondary schools to say conversion was to enable collaboration.

Changes made since conversion

➪ Academies have made a wide range of changes and change was more common in sponsored than converter academies and in secondary more than primary academies.

➪ Almost nine in ten academies have procured services

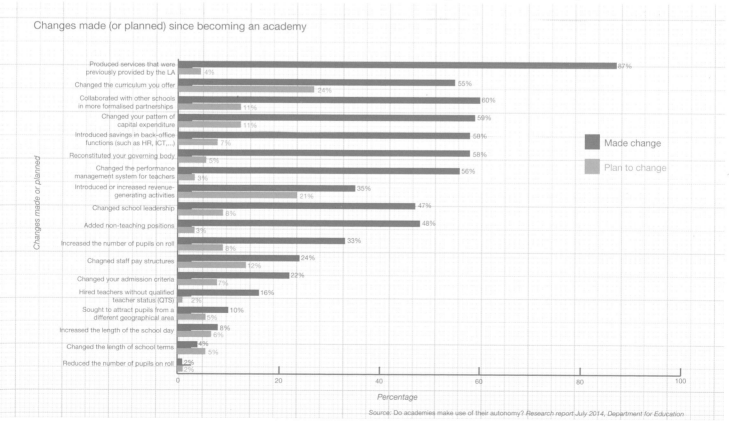

Changes made (or planned) since becoming an academy

	Made change	Plan to change
Produced services that were previously provided by the LA	87%	4%
Changed the curriculum you offer	55%	24%
Collaborated with other schools in more formalised partnerships	60%	11%
Changed your pattern of capital expenditure	59%	11%
Introduced savings in back-office functions (such as HR, ICT,...)	58%	7%
Reconstituted your governing body	58%	5%
Changed the performance management system for teachers	56%	3%
Introduced or increased revenue-generating activities	35%	21%
Changed school leadership	47%	8%
Added non-teaching positions	48%	3%
Increased the number of pupils on roll	33%	8%
Chagned staff pay structures	24%	12%
Changed your admission criteria	22%	7%
Hired teachers without qualified teacher status (QTS)	16%	2%
Sought to attract pupils from a different geographical area	10%	5%
Increased the length of the school day	8%	6%
Changed the length of school terms	4%	5%
Reduced the number of pupils on roll	2%	2%

Percentage

Source: Do academies make use of their autonomy? Research report July 2014, Department for Education

previously provided by their local authority (LA) from another source. Three quarters have changed (55 per cent) or plan to (24 per cent) change the curriculum they offer; and almost three quarters have formalised collaboration arrangements (60 per cent) or plan to (11 per cent).

⇨ Only a small proportion (14 per cent) have changed (eight per cent) or plan to (six per cent) change length of school day and nine per cent have changed (four per cent) or plan to (five per cent) change school terms.

⇨ Academies that have been open longer have made more changes. More recent openers have not yet planned to make all of the changes made by early academies.

Impact of changes made

⇨ Two thirds of academies believe that the changes they have made have improved attainment. This is especially the case for sponsored academies. The longer an academy has been open, the more likely they are to say the changes have substantially improved attainment.

⇨ Increased collaboration, changes to the curriculum and school leadership were felt to have led to the biggest improvements in academies. Changes in leadership were

seen as important especially in sponsored academies.

Use of non-QTS teachers

⇨ 16 per cent of academies have hired unqualified teachers but only five per cent of academies have any unqualified teachers who are not working towards QTS.

⇨ Those open as academies longer are more likely to have hired a non-QTS teacher.

Use of new curricula from Sept 2014

⇨ Mathematics (by 77 per cent of respondents), English (76 per cent) and Science (67 per cent) are the new curricula most likely to be used in September. Secondary academies are more likely than primary to follow the national curriculum for the majority of subjects, which suggests innovation in the primary sector.

Change in volume of first choice applications

⇨ Over half of sponsored academies (66 per cent of secondary sponsored) and a third of converters reported an increase in first choice applications since becoming an academy.

⇨ The longer an academy is open, the more likely they were to say they had experienced an increase in first choice applications.

Attitudes to borrowing funds

⇨ Views are evenly divided – a third of academies would like to be able to borrow funds, a third would not, and a third are unsure. Secondary academies are more interested in borrowing.

⇨ Schools who became academies shortly after May 2010 were more likely to be interested in borrowing funds.

School-to-school support

⇨ 87 per cent of academies support other schools (91 per cent of converters and 74 per cent of sponsored). 72 per cent of academies support schools they did not support before conversion.

⇨ Almost all academies rated outstanding by Ofsted support other schools (96 per cent).

⇨ Academies often receive support from academies within a trust of which they are not a member, whether a member of a different MAT or not.

Managing teacher performance

⇨ Over half (53 per cent) of academies have changed how they monitor teacher performance – this was most common in sponsored and secondary academies.

⇨ Around two thirds of academies monitor pupils' attainment and progress at least half-termly. Almost 90 per cent of sponsored academies do so.

⇨ 84 per cent of academies explicitly link pay to performance.

9 July 2014

⇨ The above information is reprinted with kind permission from the Department for Education. Please visit www.gov. uk for further information.

corporate sponsorship

increased school to school collaboration

teacher pay based on performance

academy school

better educational results

market-driven education

customised curriculum

Does academy conversion actually lead to slower improvement in schools?

By Henry Stewart

Last week the report of the Education Select Committee stated that 'current evidence does not allow us to draw conclusions on whether academies in themselves are a positive force for change'. It added that 'academisation is not always successful nor is it the only proven alternative for a struggling school'. This was not exactly a ringing endorsement of the academies programme, coming as it did from a committee chaired by Conservative MP Graham Stuart and with a majority of members from the Coalition.

Yet today David Cameron will announce that any school rated by Ofsted as 'Requires Improvement' or 'Inadequate' will be subject to conversion to an academy. The *Telegraph* noted that almost 4,000 schools currently have one of these ratings (though some of these are of course already academies). It is hard to see where the evidence is that this is a sensible focus or use of resources.

My extensive analysis for this site has repeatedly found that, when sponsored secondary academies are compared to similar non-academies, there is no evidence of faster improvement. This was effectively accepted by the DfE in a High Court case last summer where they claimed only that results for academies were 'marginally higher' than other similar schools – and then only if GCSE equivalents (now removed from the benchmark figure) were included.

My analysis, the detail of which has never been challenged by the DfE or their supporters, showed that once the equivalents were stripped out, sponsored academies actually performed worse than similar non-academies. The release of the 2014 GCSE data last week confirmed this with results falling much more in sponsored academies than in similar community schools.

Primary schools: the evidence shows that academy conversion slows improvement

Conversion of primary schools to academy status is more recent and, as a result, there has been less research. Indeed the Education Select Committee stated that there was 'no convincing evidence of the impact of academy status on attainment in primary schools'. At the time that it was taking evidence there had only been one year of figures for any significant number of primary academies.

However, last May the TES concluded that 'academy conversion does not raise primary test results', based on the first LSN analysis of primary academy results, comparing KS2 figures from 2012 to 2013.

The 2014 school-by-school KS2 results were released in December and so it is now possible to analyse the performance of sponsored primary academies over two years. It is clear that academy conversion leads to slower improvement in the first year of conversion. However academy proponents might have a case if the academies grew more in subsequent years. In fact the evidence is of slower growth in the first year and similar growth after that, leaving the sponsored academies behind their comparable non-academies.

The first analysis compares those schools which, at the time of the 2013 results, had been sponsored academies for at least six months. The second is for those who converted in the first six months of 2013, to see if having only jsut converted makes a difference.

Primary schools becoming sponsored academies up to end of 2012: slower growth

The DfE data on KS2 results allows us to compare the growth of sponsored academies and non-academies. To ensure similar schools are being compared, I have grouped the sets of schools by their 2012 results (as schools with a lower starting point tend to grow at a faster rate). These graphs only include primary schools with at least 25 children in Year 6, to avoid the big % changes that can happen in schools with small numbers of students.

It is clear that in the immediate period after conversion, the results of sponsored academies increase at a slower rate than similar non-academies. Non-academies in the 40–60% band grew their results by 10.8%, compared to 3.6% for sponsored academies. In the 60–80% band, the figures were 2.8% against 0.6%.

This may be because the focus on conversion, with all its complexities, takes attention away from the core work of teaching and learning. However, there is no evidence of catch-up in the year after:

In the second year (2013–2014) both sponsored academies and similar non-academies grew at a very similar rate. This means that growth over the two years remained substantially greater for those primary schools that were not converted to become academies (16.0% v 8.7% for the 40–60% band, 6.3% v 3.9% for the 60–80% band).

Note: The data for sponsored academies is based on 76 primary schools, with at least 25 children in Year 6, that became sponsored academies by the end of 2012. There were 27 in the range 40–60% and 42 in the range 60–80%. (There were also three that were below 40% and four that were above 80%, too small a number to make comparisons in those bands).

Primary schools becoming sponsored academies, first half of 2013: slower growth again

I separated out the sponsored academies that converted in the first half of 2013, as it could be argued that these would not have had time to see the 'benefits' of becoming an academy. However, the comparison is very similar to those that converted earlier:

Again, over two years, the non academies clearly improved their results at a faster rate.

Note: In this data, there were 33 sponsored academies in the 40–60% band for 2012 results and 60 in the 60–80% band (as well as four below 40% and eight above 80% in 2012).

Conclusion

David Cameron is proposing that poorly rated schools should be converted to academies. In fact the evidence shows this will slow their improvement. Instead of a massive disruption of our schools for a solution for which there is no evidence, the DfE should research – as a priority – what it is that enabled the above maintained schools to improve at such a fast rate.

Perhaps, after five years of ideology-driven structural changes to our schools, it is time for evidence-based policy.

Data notes

⇨ This analysis is solely about 'sponsored academies', which are generally conversions of 'under-achieving' schools. As David Cameron is referring to schools rated 'Inadequate' or 'Requires Improvement', these will become sponsored academies. The other category is 'converter academies', which covers the conversion of schools that were generally already successful.

⇨ 2014 KS2 data: DfE school and college performance tables (http://www.education.gov.uk/schools/performance/index.html).

⇨ Academies, with conversion date: Open academies and academies in development (https://www.gov.uk/government/publications/open-academies-and-academy-projects-in-development).

⇨ A school is treated by the DfE as a new school after conversion and the tables do not include previous results as a maintained school. The analysis therefore involved using the information in the academies spreadsheet (which includes the reference number of its previous school) to link results as an academy and as its predecessor school. Sponsored academies which are the outcome of two predecessor schools are not included in the analysis.

2 February 2015

⇨ The above information is reprinted with kind permission from the Local Schools Network. Please visit www.localschoolsnetwork.org.uk for further information.

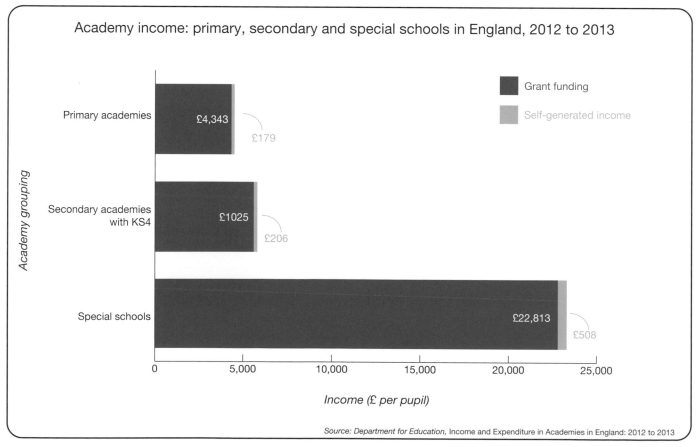

Academy income: primary, secondary and special schools in England, 2012 to 2013

Legend: Grant funding, Self-generated income

- Primary academies: £4,343 / £179
- Secondary academies with KS4: £1025 / £206
- Special schools: £22,813 / £508

Y-axis: Academy grouping
X-axis: Income (£ per pupil) — 0, 5,000, 10,000, 15,000, 20,000, 25,000

Source: Department for Education, Income and Expenditure in Academies in England: 2012 to 2013

Free Schools: the basics

Free Schools are new independent state-funded schools. Drawing on the experience of international new school programmes, they provide a way for groups of parents, teachers, charities, existing schools or other organisations to respond to a need for a new school in their community – whether for extra places, to raise standards or offer choice.

Like all state schools, Free Schools are free to attend and open to all children. They have been opened all over England by parents, teachers, existing outstanding schools, community groups and charities. They can be primary, secondary, all-through or 16–19. They can also be focused specifically for children with special educational needs or those who struggle in mainstream schools (alternative provision).

Setting up a new school is a challenging and rigorous process. Groups have to demonstrate to the Department for Education that they have excellent educational expertise and a strong team that is capable of responsibly governing a school. They also have to prove that there is demand for the school in their community and show that they have developed a detailed education plan that will meet the needs of their students.

Once established, Free Schools are legally Academies so are funded by central government and have a range of freedoms.

⇨ They do not have to teach the National Curriculum but are required to teach a broad and balanced curriculum with a focus on the core subjects of English, Maths and Science: some schools use this freedom to teach different curricula – whether that is a challenging international maths curriculum or taking a different approach to learning with a theme each term linking all subjects.

⇨ They can extend the school day or year: most use this freedom to add more time for learning or extra-curricular activity.

⇨ They have more flexibility in the way they employ their staff: some choose to offer teachers performance-related pay to keep and reward their best staff while others choose to bring in outside expertise by employing people without traditional teaching qualifications.

⇨ They decide how they spend their full budget: they receive all of their funding direct from central government, which means they have complete independence over how it is spent

⇨ They have independent governance: Free Schools are run by an Academy Trust, and are independent of local authority oversight. Therefore the role of governors in overseeing an open school is particularly important.

Did you know?

Free Schools have to prove that they are wanted by parents and students before they are allowed to be set up. You cannot set up a Free School without local demand whilst Special and Alternative Provision schools have to prove they would be sent pupils by local schools and local authorities. These local needs are very varied but usually include one or more of the following:

Shortage of school places

Often there are simply not enough school places in a particular area. For many parents, getting access to their first choice, or even just a good local school, has become a lottery. For those that cannot afford to move house to get into desirable catchment areas choice can be very limited and a new school can be the perfect solution.

Raise standards or offer a different choice

Many Free School groups are created because existing schools in their area are not performing well and they want to raise standards locally.

Sometimes parents also want a different choice locally, perhaps a school with a science specialism, bilingual teaching, a particular faith ethos or a focus on music or sport. Read some of our individual Free School stories to see the wide variety of schools that have opened (visit http://www.newschoolsnetwork. org/what-are-free-schools/inside-free-schools). At both primary and secondary level, the opening of a Free School has led to gains in performance of the lowest performing schools nearby.

Unique support for students with particular needs

Around one in seven Free Schools have been created to support students with a particular need. This could be children with special educational needs or for those on the verge of exclusion who are not getting the support they need in existing mainstream schools. For example, over 2,200 new places have been created in Free Schools for children with autism while charities like Southend YMCA and Everton in the Community have created 'alternative provision' schools for students at risk of exclusion.

Support the most deprived

Many of the charities, schools, teachers and parents involved in setting up Free Schools are particularly passionate about making sure their school brings the biggest benefits to the most deprived communities: Free Schools are ten times more likely to be located in the most deprived areas in England than in the least deprived.

⇨ The above information is reprinted with kind permission from New Schools Network. Please visit http://www. newschoolsnetwork.org for further information.

© New Schools Network 2015

Promoting fundamental British values as part of SMSC in schools

Departmental advice for maintained schools from the Department for Education.

Fundamental British values

Schools should promote the fundamental British values of democracy, the rule of law, individual liberty, and mutual respect and tolerance of those with different faiths and beliefs.[1] This can help schools to demonstrate how they are meeting the requirements of section 78 of the Education Act 2002, in their provision of SMSC.

Actively promoting the values means challenging opinions or behaviours in school that are contrary to fundamental British values. Attempts to promote systems that undermine fundamental British values would be completely at odds with schools' duty to provide SMSC. The Teachers' Standards expect teachers to uphold public trust in the profession and maintain high standards of ethics and behaviour, within and outside school. This includes not undermining fundamental British values.

Through their provision of SMSC, schools should:

⇨ enable students to develop their self-knowledge, self-esteem and self-confidence;

⇨ enable students to distinguish right from wrong and to respect the civil and criminal law of England;

⇨ encourage students to accept responsibility for their behaviour, show initiative, and to understand how they can contribute positively to the lives of those living and working in the locality of the school and to society more widely;

⇨ enable students to acquire a broad general knowledge of and respect for public institutions and services in England;

⇨ further tolerance and harmony between different cultural

traditions by enabling students to acquire an appreciation of and respect for their own and other cultures;

⇨ encourage respect for other people; and

⇨ encourage respect for democracy and support for participation in the democratic processes, including respect for the basis on which the law is made and applied in England.

The list below describes the understanding and knowledge expected of pupils as a result of schools promoting fundamental British values.

⇨ an understanding of how citizens can influence decision-making through the democratic process;

⇨ an appreciation that living under the rule of law protects individual citizens and is essential for their well-being and safety;

⇨ an understanding that there is a separation of power between the executive and the judiciary, and that while some public bodies such as the police and the army can be held to account through Parliament, others such as the courts maintain independence;

⇨ an understanding that the freedom to choose and hold other faiths and beliefs is protected in law;

⇨ an acceptance that other people having different faiths or beliefs to oneself (or having none) should be accepted and tolerated, and should not be the cause of prejudicial or discriminatory behaviour; and

⇨ an understanding of the importance of identifying and combatting discrimination. It is not necessary for schools or individuals to 'promote' teachings, beliefs or opinions that conflict with their own, but nor is it

acceptable for schools to promote discrimination against people or groups on the basis of their belief, opinion or background.

Examples of actions that a school can take

The following is not designed to be exhaustive, but provides a list of different actions that schools can take, such as:

⇨ include in suitable parts of the curriculum, as appropriate for the age of pupils, material on the strengths, advantages and disadvantages of democracy, and how democracy and the law works in Britain, in contrast to other forms of government in other countries;

⇨ ensure that all pupils within the school have a voice that is listened to, and demonstrate how democracy works by actively promoting democratic processes such as a school council whose members are voted for by the pupils;

⇨ use opportunities such as general or local elections to hold mock elections to promote fundamental British values and provide pupils with the opportunity to learn how to argue and defend points of view;

⇨ use teaching resources from a wide variety of sources to help pupils understand a range of faiths, and

⇨ consider the role of extra-curricular activity, including any run directly by pupils, in promoting fundamental British values.

November 2014

⇨ The above information is reprinted with kind permission from the Department for Education. Please visit www.gov.uk for further information.

© Crown copyright 2015

1 The Prevent strategy 2011: https://www.gov.uk/government/publications/prevent-strategy-2011

Progress in getting all children to school stalls but some countries show the way forward

This paper, jointly released by the Education for All Global Monitoring Report (GMR) and the UNESCO Institute for Statistics (UIS), shows that global progress in reducing the number of children out of school has come to a virtual standstill. But many countries have made major progress since 2000 and offer examples to follow.

Global progress towards universal primary education has halted

As debate continues over the goals and targets of the post-2015 development agenda, new data show that the world will not fulfil one of the most basic commitments: to get every child in school by 2015. According to UIS data, nearly 58 million children of primary school age (typically between six and 11 years of age) were not enrolled in school in 2012. Many of them will probably never enter a classroom.

The momentum to reach out-of-school children has slowed considerably in recent years, with the global primary out-of-school rate stuck at 9% since 2007. This marks a stark contrast to progress at the start of the decade, when the international community pledged to achieve universal primary education (UPE) at the World Education Forum in 2000. The standstill at the global level is the result of opposing trends: a significant decline in the number of out-of-school children in certain countries due to important policy initiatives, and a rising school-age population in sub-Saharan Africa. In view of the most recent UIS data, it is certain that the world will not reach the goal of UPE by 2015.

Progress has slowed mainly because the number of children out of school in sub-Saharan Africa remained at about 30 million between 2007 and 2012. As a result, the share of the world's out-of-school children living in sub-Saharan Africa has increased to more than one-half of the total in the most recent years with data. By contrast, South and West Asia has made considerable gains, reducing the number of out-of-school children by two-thirds from 34 million in 2000 to ten million in 2012. The share of girls in the total number of out-of-school children in South and West Asia fell from two-thirds in 2000 to less than one-half in 2012. In sub-Saharan Africa, on the other hand, the female proportion of the total out-of-school population increased slightly between 2000 and 2012, from 54% to 56%.

India, Indonesia, Niger, Nigeria, Pakistan and Sudan each have more than one million children out of school. The graph presents data for countries facing the greatest challenges, although it is important to note that this list is not exhaustive. Countries such as Afghanistan and Somalia are also struggling to provide every child with a primary education but lack the data to provide accurate counts of their out-of-school populations.

There is also a growing demand for secondary education as more countries approach UPE. UIS data provide information on educational exclusion among adolescents of lower secondary school age, typically between 12 and 15 years of age. In 2012, 63 million young adolescents around the world were not enrolled in primary or secondary school, compared with 97 million in 2000. South and West Asia has the biggest share of this population with 26 million out-of-school adolescents, although this represents a reduction by nearly one-third since 2000. Progress in the region has been especially notable for girls since 2000, when nearly three in five out-of-school children were female, compared to less than one-half in 2012. The second-highest number is found in sub-Saharan Africa (21 million), where there has been almost no change in gender parity since the beginning of the last decade. Across the region, girls account for 54% of

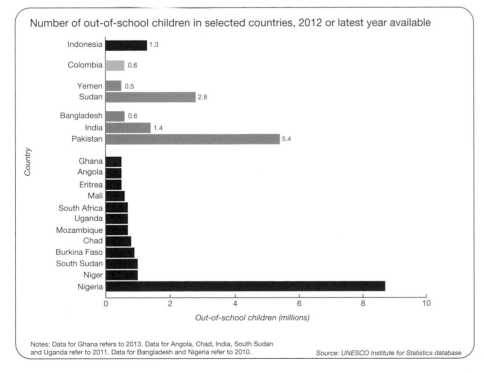

Number of out-of-school children in selected countries, 2012 or latest year available

Country / Out-of-school children (millions)

Indonesia 1.3
Colombia 0.6
Yemen 0.5
Sudan 2.8
Bangladesh 0.6
India 1.4
Pakistan 5.4
Ghana
Angola
Eritrea
Mali
South Africa
Uganda
Mozambique
Chad
Burkina Faso
South Sudan
Niger
Nigeria

Notes: Data for Ghana refers to 2013. Data for Angola, Chad, India, South Sudan and Uganda refer to 2011. Data for Bangladesh and Nigeria refer to 2010.

Source: UNESCO Institute for Statistics database

the total adolescent out-of-school population compared with 57% in 2000.

More than four out of ten out-of-school children will never enter a classroom

While access to education has been improving globally, there has been little progress in reducing the rate at which children leave school before reaching the last grade of primary education. About 135 million children began primary school in 2012, but if current trends continue 34 million children (some older than the official school age) will leave school before reaching the last grade of primary. The early school leaving rate of 25% has remained at the same level as in 2000. To achieve UPE, new interventions are required to reduce this rate.

Sub-Saharan Africa and South and West Asia have the highest rates of early school leaving. Across these regions, more than one in every three students who started primary school in 2012 will not make it to the last grade.

To better gauge how the out-of-school numbers are related to early school leaving, the UIS identifies three groups of out-of-school children of primary school age according to their exposure to education: those who have left school early, those who are expected to enter school in the future and those who are expected to never attend school.

Of the 58 million out-of-school children of primary age, 23% have some schooling but dropped out. A further 34% are expected to enter school in the near future, and a full 43% will probably never enter school. Data show large variations in regional patterns. In Central Asia, South and West Asia, and sub-Saharan Africa, most out-of-school children will probably never receive any formal education. This is the case for 43% of children out of school in the Arab States. In Central and Eastern Europe, Latin America and the Caribbean, and North America and Western Europe, most out-of-school children will start school late. East Asia and the Pacific and South and West Asia have large shares of early school leavers.

The classification of out-of-school children by past and possible future school attendance yields important insights for policymakers. If the majority of out-of-school children in a country attended but left school, demand-oriented programmes and interventions should focus on reducing the dropout rate by improving the quality of education and addressing issues such as the direct and indirect costs of education. For children who are likely to attend school in the future, the goal is to ensure earlier entry into the education system.

Children who are expected to never gain access to schooling – roughly 15 million girls and ten million boys – pose serious challenges to policymakers.

Addressing the issue of out-of-school children means improving both demand and supply of education provision and requires a robust base of evidence derived from the latest data and research on out-of-school children.

Some countries have shown the way forward

While the world on average appears to have lost steam in its effort to ensure that all children are in school, some countries have demonstrated that rapid progress is possible within a relatively short period of time. Other data shows countries that had at least 100,000 out-of-school children in 2000 and managed to reduce those populations by at least 50% by 2012 or the latest year available with data. Together these 17 countries, which accounted for about one-quarter of the global out-of-school population in 2000, managed to reduce their out-of-school numbers by 86%, from 27 million to less than four million, in little over a decade.

For example, 24% of children of primary school age were out of school in Nepal in 2000; by 2013, the rate had fallen to just 1% with the out-of-school population falling by 660,000. Likewise in Morocco, the out-of-school population fell by 96%, or more than 930,000, between 2000 and 2013. How did they achieve this remarkable feat? What policies were used to translate political will into effective action?

The remainder of the paper looks at the paths followed in 11 of these countries from five regions, for which complementary survey data are available. These survey data show that the percentage of children who had never been to school also fell by at least 50% roughly between 2000 and 2010 in eight of these 11 countries.

June 2014

⇨ The above information is reprinted with kind permission from the Education for All Global Monitoring Report (GMR) and the UNESCO Institute for Statistics (UIS). Please visit www.efareport.unesco.org for further information.

What will the classroom of the future look like?

By Dominic Sacco

Imagine your local school doesn't have a single classroom; children are all connected to the Internet and the teachers have been replaced by apps.

It's a scenario that's not as far-fetched as you might believe. Schools are already incredibly tech-savvy with smartboards, tablets and faster Internet becoming the norm – and networking specialist Cisco expects IoT (the Internet of Things, or connected devices and objects) to have a greater influence on schools.

'The classroom of the future may not even be a room,' says Sarah Eccleston, director of enterprise networks and IoT at Cisco UK and Ireland.

'It can become much more of a remote virtual learning environment where you can use video much more greatly, and everything and everybody can be connected to the Internet. So that means you can conduct training at a distance. You can bring in experts on demand. There could be one topic but thousands of pupils that can learn the topic in the way that best suits them from a library of content.

'We have to move away from this idea of a physical classroom with a desk at the front, one teacher and rows of desks and children. The teacher might not even be a person – it could be an app on a tablet. Lessons may be conducted in a way where the teacher is more of a coach.'

Steve Woollett, Cisco's head of collaboration for the public sector in Ireland, asks: 'Can video really be better than being there? Well if you're sat watching someone getting a haircut in real life, you can only see one view. With video, you've got a shot of the front, back, sides, top – you can truly see how they're getting their hair cut.

'So in a hair cutting class, for example, rather than making notes with pens and paper, students take out their phones, take a picture of the whiteboard and carry on watching. It's a really simple but effective way of capturing that information.'

While 'live' lessons haven't quite become the norm (yet), new technology is emerging all the time. Schools already use a host of products from computers to projectors and even 3D printers, while other devices like robots and an 'iWall' are on the horizon.

More than 200 UK schools are even using a customised version of the popular computer game Minecraft, with the idea that its expansive world will help children with creative writing.

The Future Classroom Lab in Brussels is also experimenting with the teaching of the future, with its green screen broadcasting studio, plus a whiteboard that can be extended horizontally for group work.

Connected kids

So how will the Internet of Things change classrooms in the future? The potential in this area is huge, with teachers able to track changes in the quality of soil by connecting a special sensor device, for example. This could have an impact on science lessons as children grow plants. But it won't just be objects that connect to the Internet.

'The teachers are connected to the Internet, the things you're teaching children about are connected to the Internet, so you can have more interactive ways of learning, and also you can start to connect some of the pupils to the Internet too,' explains Sarah Eccleston.

'And for those with learning difficulties or ADHD, a headset has been created with sensors that can connect to the Internet and detect brain activity. It can see when that pupil is concentrating and actually learning. So this can help improve the standard of education.

'You can also connect things not just to the Internet but to each other. So now you can have a collaboration between schools over certain topics. You can start to do better project

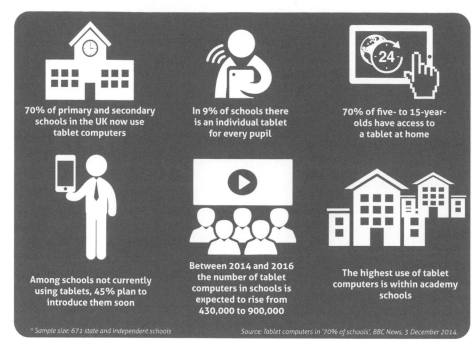

70% of primary and secondary schools in the UK now use tablet computers

In 9% of schools there is an individual tablet for every pupil

70% of five- to 15-year-olds have access to a tablet at home

Among schools not currently using tablets, 45% plan to introduce them soon

Between 2014 and 2016 the number of tablet computers in schools is expected to rise from 430,000 to 900,000

The highest use of tablet computers is within academy schools

Sample size: 671 state and independent schools   Source: Tablet computers in '70% of schools', BBC News, 3 December 2014.

work, for example you can connect those with archeology interests together and connect them to sites and digs, and connect those with the same skill level and interests together. Even if they're in different schools and countries.'

But with all this data comes a number of safety and security issues.

Steve Woollett says: 'There are apps now where head teachers or supervisors can log on via their PC or Mac and see in real time what kids are seeing on their screen. And if there's something inappropriate, they can send them a message or cut it off.'

Sarah Eccleston adds: 'It's also about physical security. Cisco has other technology that connects to the Internet like cameras and sensors. Security officers can pre-configure the school's cameras remotely, so they can monitor crime, and they've got really good coverage of entrants and exits, parking lots and storage facilities.'

When will live lessons and the Internet of things in schools go mainstream?

'Well, the technology is there now – it's a just a case of more schools wanting to adopt it,' Eccleston explains.

'The connection of everything to the Internet will happen in the classroom as it happens in other areas of the community as well. It's at the stage at the moment where it's starting to happen, and although we can't predict when it will happen fully, when it does it will be a tidal wave.'

Six new tech products for schools

Bakerboard

Created by Clifford Dax, the Bakerboard is a traditional prototype board paired with an electronics suite.

Designed for science classes, students can play about with the oscilloscope, spectral display, function generator and power supply to learn more about circuits.

The Bakerboard was successfully funded on Kickstarter in July, receiving twice the amount of its $5,000 target.

Hummingbird Duo

After the huge success of the Raspberry Pi, there has been a number of other mini PCs that have followed.

The latest one, the Hummingbird Duo, comes in the form of robotics kits specifically designed to take students through a series of levels, rather than just giving them a mini PC and letting them figure out what to do with it.

Oculus Rift

So far the Oculus Rift has mainly been aimed at gamers, but new research from game development studio Dubit has found that students aged between seven and 12 years old want to use the headset in schools.

'Without prompting, all children said they thought virtual reality would be great in their schools,' said head of research Peter Robinson. 'They thought it would make lessons more interesting and allow them to take "virtual field trips".'

Kibo

As programming becomes a more important part of the curriculum, tech companies are looking to make products for specific age groups. KinderLab Robotics has produced the KIBO for children aged four to seven years old. It's a robot kit designed to look and work like a traditional wooden toy, requiring no PC, tablet or smartphone.

The child can create a series of instructions using wooden blocks, which are scanned by a robot that then performs the actions.

Pepper

Recently launched in Japan, Pepper is an 'emotionally aware' robot designed to perform a range of tasks.

Its 'emotional engine' is powered by a cloud-based AI system and can gauge the emotions of people around it. For example, if a child is sad, Pepper can recognise this and try to cheer it up. Manufacturer Aldebaran has already deployed 5,000 robots worldwide across various research, education and care programmes.

iWall

As tablets and interactive whiteboards become commonplace in the classroom, it may only be a matter of time until interactive video walls such as MultiTaction's iWall make their way to schools.

The iWall is described as a social experience, designed to get users collaborating with each other. The iWall comprises of 12 55-inch ultra thin displays with 24MP resolution.

11 August 2014

⇨ The above information is reprinted with kind permission from PCR – the UK trade publication for computer and IT resellers, retailers, system builders, distributors and vendors. Please visit www.pcr-online.biz for further information.

Believe the hype: e-learning can revolutionise education in Africa

Rebecca Stromeyer who runs the annual e-learning Africa conference tells us how IT is transforming education.

By Natricia Duncan

Tell us a bit about yourself

My father was an educational entrepreneur who always encouraged me to take an active role in the family business. In 1975 we were living in Lebanon, but we were forced to flee when the country descended into civil war. We essentially became refugees in the UK. Challenging times followed. At 15 I was living in an apartment with just my younger sister. But one of the things that kept me focused and grounded was my early education. So I know first hand the value of learning.

The initial idea for the e-learning events was sparked in 2004 when I heard about optical fibre cables being laid in Ethiopia. I realised the potential information and communications technologies (ICT) held for development in Africa. This year's eLearning Africa conference in Uganda is our ninth. We have been hosted by Ethiopia, Kenya, Ghana, Tanzania, Zambia, Senegal, Benin and Namibia and typically have over 1,500 participants and more than 300 speakers.

How do your conferences support development?

Learning is the cornerstone of all development. Without the underpinning of quality education, other systems upon which development depends – governance, health, economic growth, the judiciary, commerce – can never reach maturity.

Our e-learning conferences bring together stakeholders from every sector: government, private organisations and bodies like the United Nations Organisation for Education, Science and Culture (UNESCO) – techie people can meet academics and everyone in between, and cooperate on development issues.

But one of our priorities is getting the grassroots workers to the conference. So we award scholarships and subsidies, because it is important that we give people like teachers and headteachers a voice, to gain an understanding of the deeper issues. We also connect them with policymakers and organisations who want to support them, whether through funding or providing materials like computers.

This networking happens on a number of levels, so a minister from Malawi might connect with a minister from Ghana and they can learn from each other. We try to highlight, not just what is best practice, but also what is worst practice, because part of the solution is knowing what not to do.

With 30 million children out of school in sub-Saharan Africa, the region has been identified as a priority area for Unesco. How can ICT help to address the problem?

An African permanent secretary once told me that e-learning is the solution for education in Africa. I pointed out that I come from a generation that was schooled without that technology and is extremely well educated. What is vital, I argued, is adequate teacher training. But e-learning is also very important, especially in the Internet, technology-driven world we live in.

For Africa it can be a valuable tool in improving access to education. For example, to produce textbooks and distribute them across schools

is hugely expensive and very difficult. Whereas online access to information such as teaching resources and lesson plans, which can be used to build a curriculum, is cheap and easy once the technology and infrastructure is in place and the teacher is trained to use it.

What are some of the themes in this year's conference?

One of the main themes is the youth. There is a skills deficit that is preventing them from progressing and we want to open a discussion on ways to address this.

We will also discuss whether Africa should adopt a western higher education model or create different kinds of programmes. Also, how to use technology to attract young people to working in agriculture. And we want to connect the many new African IT entrepreneurs with policymakers, so governments know what tools or infrastructure they need to enhance and support what they are doing.

What are some of the challenges facing the organisation?

One of our main challenges is trying to keep ahead of trends while also trying to maintain a balance and not get swept up in empty hype. There are a lot of hot topics in the education-technology sector at the moment, and while we need to reflect these changes in our conference programmes, there is a danger of losing sight of the less rock star basic elements, which may often be more impactful in the long term.

What is your vision for the organisation?

To continue to be a great enabler for development in Africa, to raise awareness of what can be done and give people access to the information and technology to accomplish it. It is also important to get governments to realise the value of teachers and ensure they have the tools and environment they need to do their jobs. Education is the key to understanding and democracy, and in Africa it is a vital tool for development and empowerment.

26 May 2014

⇨ The above information is reprinted with kind permission from *The Guardian*. Please visit www.theguardian.com for further information.

EU Children of Peace: educating children affected by conflict in Ethiopia

Save the Children's latest project aimed at educating children in emergencies will see over 5,400 children gain access to basic education, many for the first time. It's funded by the European Union's Children of Peace Initiative using, in part, money awarded to the EU as winner of the 2012 Nobel Peace Prize.

Education in conflict

Today, there are over 28 million children out of school in countries affected by conflict and fragility.

And these children regularly tell us is that what they want most is to go back to school.

Each and every child should have the opportunity to receive an education, develop their talents and grow up in peace. Ultimately, when a conflict breaks out it is the context that changes, not a child's need for education.

Education is crucial for both the protection and the development of children affected by conflict and by promoting education we can give children affected by conflict new hope for the future.

Save the Children is setting up temporary schools and learning spaces in the Dollo Ado refugee camp in Ethiopia. Dollo Ado is home to almost 200,000 refugees from Somalia – 69% are children and of those 95% have had no formal education in their homeland.

Our project will also train teachers and other community leaders and provide essential teaching materials such as books, stationery, learning materials and educational play materials.

As well as getting an education our schools and learning spaces will mean children have access to other key lifesaving services such as health, nutrition, hygiene and school feeding programmes. There will also be child protection services that identify and protect children from the threats and risks they face associated with living in refugee camps.

EU Children of Peace

The EU Children of Peace initiative is funded by the one million euro 2012 Nobel Peace Prize award, plus a matching contribution from ECHO, the EU's humanitarian agency.

Save the Children joint project with the Norwegian Refugee Council (NRC) to help 14,000 children affected by conflict in Somalia and the Democratic Republic of Congo (DRC) was one of four projects chosen to recieve EU Children of Peace funding. The NRC project is focusing on 9,000 children displaced by the fighting in eastern DRC.

Why education in emergencies?

⇨ Education is a recognised right – learning cannot and should not be put aside in times of crisis as education is crucial to children and young people's futures

⇨ Education protects children from physical, emotional and psychological harm during emergencies, minimising the risk of abuse, exploitation and harm

⇨ Education can promote peace, stability and social cohesion, which reduces the risk of future conflict and helps reduce poverty and inequality

⇨ Education is essential to children's social and emotional development and provides a sense of normality in an otherwise chaotic world

⇨ Education can provide entry points for other life-saving interventions, including protection, water and sanitation, health and nutrition and should be part of all integrated responses

⇨ Children, youths, parents and communities continue to prioritise education, especially during an emergency

What are we doing?

Democratic Republic of Congo

After decades of conflict, the eastern provinces of the DRC continue to be affected by massive displacement. The recent escalation of violence in 2012 has resulted in over 750,000 people living in displacement in North Kivu Province alone. With the majority of those displaced living in camps, many children are now suffering the effects of a situation they have no control over.

It is estimated that less than 40% of children living in displacement camps are enrolled in some sort of education scheme, this figure drops as low as 20% for those living in spontaneous sites around the camps. With tens of thousands of children not attending school, exposure to armed groups and other risks are extremely high.

As part of the Children of Peace initiative the Norwegian Refugee Council will reach some 9,180 children affected by conflict in Nord Kivu Province, DRC.

As part of the project:

⇨ 7,180 children will be given afternoon catch-up classes to make up for the time they have spent outside of the education system

⇨ School supply kits including textbooks, notepads, stationery and school equipment will be distributed benefitting 7,180 students and 234 teachers across 12 schools

⇨ 2,000 children and youth will have access to extra-curricular and recreational activities in two newly built Temporary Learning Spaces

⇨ Mobility aids will be provided to children with physical disabilities

⇨ A school destroyed after ethnic clashes will be completely rebuilt and equipped to ensure that children are able to attend lessons

⇨ Teachers and community volunteers will receive training on child protection, sanitation and other public health messages

Ethiopia

There are now over 190,000 Somali refugees living in the Dollo Ado refugee camps in Ethiopia. Over 69% are under the age of 18.

Yet, very few of these are enrolled in the education system. In the 2011/2012 academic year only one in four school-aged boys and girls in the camps where Save the Children was already working were enrolled in school.

Save the Children have been working in Dollo Ado, responding to the influx of refugees from Somalia, since 2009 and our Early Childhood Care and Development programme already enrols some 10,000 children aged three to six across the camps.

Thanks to the EU's Children of Peace initiative, Save the Children will be able to reach a further 5,400 children between the ages of 11–14. This funding will:

⇨ Allow 5,400 children to access Alternative Basic Education (ABE) classes where the curriculum is condensed into three levels in order for children to complete it in a shorter timeframe

⇨ Ensure that 5,400 children have direct access to Child Friendly Spaces where they can get involved in extra-curricular activities and have a safe space to play

⇨ Establish 20 ABE classes and train 135 literacy and numeracy community volunteers to ensure greater access to education in the camp

⇨ Ensure that 5,400 children will have the right equipment to go to school through the distribution of schoolbag kits that include stationery and learning materials

June 2013

⇨ The above information is reprinted with kind permission from Save the Children. Please visit www.savethechildren.org.uk for further information.

Key facts

⇨ In the UK state system, children start primary school at the age of five. (page 1)

⇨ In Europe, the most common school starting age is six, and even seven in some cases such as Finland. (page 8)

⇨ In a 2004 longitudinal study of 3,000 children funded by the Department of Education itself, Oxford's Kathy Sylva and colleagues showed that an extended period of high-quality, play-based pre-school education made a significant difference to academic learning and well-being through the primary school years. (page 9)

⇨ In April to June 2014 eight per cent of people aged 16 to 18 were not in education, employment or training, the lowest second-quarter figure since records began in 2000. (page 10)

⇨ Just over half of all students who failed to get grades A* to C in English or maths in 2011 stayed in school to try and retake them, but the figures show that only 6.5% eventually achieved this standard in English and only 7% in maths. (page 11)

⇨ In the survey of 291 companies employing nearly 1.5 million people, over half (61%) are concerned about the resilience and self-management of school leavers and a third (33%) with their attitude to work. (page 12)

⇨ Among employers with links to schools and colleges, the most common forms of support are offering work experience placements (77%) and providing careers advice and talks (67%). (page 13)

⇨ More than half of young people (55%) aged 11–16 say they would be interested in an apprenticeship rather than going to university if it was available in a job they wanted to do, but only 30% say that their teachers have ever discussed the idea of apprenticeships with them at school (Ipsos MORI, 11–16- year-olds). (page 14)

⇨ 56% of parents say they are likely to encourage their children to go for a degree, while only 40% would encourage them to do an apprenticeship. (page 14)

⇨ The Government's own estimates indicate the size of outstanding student debt will increase to more than £330 billion by 2044. (page 15)

⇨ Marking was one of the biggest issues for teachers; 32% of respondents said that modifying marking arrangements would be a good way to make a real difference to their workloads. (page 18)

⇨ Results of a freedom of information (FOI) request, published by leading children's charity the National Children's Bureau (NCB), suggest that on any given day as many as 14,800 children are missing education in England. (page 22)

⇨ By four or five, healthy children can normally say 1,500 to 2,000 words. (page 23)

⇨ More than two-thirds (70%) of parents say they have struggled with the cost of school. This rises to 95% of parents who live in families that are 'not well off at all'. (page 24)

⇨ A third of children who said their family is 'not well off at all' have fallen behind in class because their family could not afford the necessary books or materials. (page 25)

⇨ Schools which converted to academy status shortly after May 2010 were more likely to do so for financial gain. More recent converters are more likely to do so for opportunities for collaboration. (page 27)

⇨ Around one in seven Free Schools have been created to support students with a particular need. This could be children with special educational needs or for those on the verge of exclusion who are not getting the support they need in existing mainstream schools. (page 31)

⇨ Sub-Saharan Africa and South and West Asia have the highest rates of early school leaving. Across these regions, more than one in every three students who started primary school in 2012 will not make it to the last grade. (page 34)

⇨ 70% of primary and secondary schools in the UK now use tablet computers. (page 36)

⇨ Today, there are over 28 million children out of school in countries affected by conflict and fragility. (page 38)

Academy

Academies (under the Academies Bill 2010) are schools that are state-maintained, but independently run and funded by external sponsors. This gives the school greater freedom from local authority bureaucracy: for example how much they pay their staff and the subjects students are taught. Often, failing state schools are encouraged to apply for academy status.

A-levels

These are qualifications usually taken by students aged 16 to 18 at schools and sixth-form colleges, although they can be taken at any time by school leavers at local colleges or through distance learning. They provide an accepted route to degree courses and university and usually take two years to complete.

Apprenticeship

A form of vocational training which involves learning a trade or skill through working. An apprentice will often shadow an experienced practitioner of a trade, learning the occupation `on the job`. Some apprenticeships can take many years.

Comprehensive school

Also known as state schools, comprehensive schools are the state-run, Government-funded schools in Britain. Education is free in comprehensive schools.

Free school

Free schools the same freedoms and flexibilities as academies, but they do not normally replace an existing school. Free schools may be set up by a wide range of proposers - including charities, universities, businesses, educational groups, teachers and groups of parents.

Further education

Education for 16- to 18-years-olds, for example college or sixth form.

GCSE

This stands for General Certificate of Secondary Education; it is the national exam taken by 16-year-olds in England and Wales. The Scottish equivalent is the Scottish Certificate of Education.

Higher education

Post-18 education, for example university.

International Baccalaureate (IB or IBac)

An alternative to A-levels, the IBac was developed in Switzerland and is highly regarded by Universities.

IGCSE

Introduced in 1988, International GCSE is an alternative to the traditional GCSEs, offered by Cambridge and Edexcel exam boards.

National Curriculum

The statutory set of guidelines set down by the Government which determine the subject material and attainment targets taught in schools in England and Wales. The National Curriculum applies to pupils up to the age of 16.

Sixth form

Sixth form is a type of post-16 education which enables students to study for their A-levels or equivalents. Some sixth-form institutions are independent colleges, whilst others are attached to secondary schools.

Students` union

Every university has a students` union: an organisation that is run by students, for students. Student unions usually offer a variety of social and sporting opportunities as well as practical services such as help groups and advice centres.

UCAS

The Universities and Colleges Admissions Service. This organisation is responsible for organising applications to higher education institutions in the UK. Prospective students do not apply to universities directly, but via UCAS.

Vocational

A qualification which is relevant to a particular career and can be expected to provide a route into that career.

Vocational learning

Education that provides practical training for a specific occupation or vocation, for example agriculture, carpentry or beauty therapy. Traditionally this is delivered through `hands-on` experience rather than academic learning, although there may be a combination of these elements depending on the course.

Assignments

Brainstorming

⇨ In small groups, discuss what you know about education in the UK. Consider the following points:

- What kinds of schools are there in the UK?
- What exams do pupils have to sit in the UK?
- What do you know about free schools and academies?

Research

⇨ Do some research about the schools in your local area. Choose a school and investigate how it differs from your own – write some notes and feedback to your class.

⇨ Find out about the differences between IGCSE, IBac and GCSE. Write some notes that explain your findings.

⇨ Look at some education-based news stories from the last two weeks. What issues are currently being discussed and how would these affect you and your school? Write some notes and then discuss in small groups.

⇨ In pairs, create a questionnaire that will be distributed to the teachers in your school. Your aim is to find out how they feel about their stress levels, and workload, and what could be done to improve their day-to-day experience of working at your school. When you receive your teachers' responses, write a report that analyses your findings and include graphs or infographics to help visualise the results. Remember the questionnaires should be anonymous.

⇨ Schools and colleges often focus on academic paths for students – providing information and encouragement for them to enter higher education. Carry out research into other opportunities in your area. Can you find any apprenticeships on offer? Or many employment vacancies suitable for a school leaver? Write a list of your findings and compare them with others in your class.

Design

⇨ Design a poster that will raise awareness of teachers' high workloads and stress levels.

⇨ Choose one of the articles in this book and create an illustration to highlight the key themes/message of your chosen article.

⇨ Design a leaflet that the difference between IGCSE, A-levels and the International Baccalaureate.

⇨ In groups, imagine that you have been given a Government grant to start your own free school. Think of a name for your school and create a manifesto that details your ethos and aims. You could include drawings/plans of classrooms, sample logos or uniforms... get creative!

Oral

⇨ 'At five years old, children are far too young to start school.' Divide your class into two groups and stage a debate in which half of the class agrees with this statement, and half disagrees.

⇨ Look at the *Compulsory age of starting school* map on page eight and choose a country where the age that children start school is different from your own. With a partner, research the education system in that country and create a two-minute presentation to share with your class.

⇨ As a class, discuss what you think the classroom of the future might look like.

⇨ Choose an illustration from this book and, in pairs, discuss what you think the artist was trying to portray in this image.

Reading/writing

⇨ Find out about the use of digital technology for education in developing countries. Write two-pages exploring your findings.

⇨ Read the article *Employers want education system to better prepare young people for life outside school gates*. Do you believe that schools do enough to provide pupils with the 'skills, character and attitudes students need to progress in life'? Write a blog post exploring your opinion.

⇨ Choose a country from the graph *Number of out-of-school children in selected countries, 2012 or latest year available*. Research the education system in your chosen country and write a report summarising your findings. You could include graphs or images to support your writing.

⇨ Write a one-paragraph definition of education poverty.

⇨ Visit *The Guardian* website and read one of the articles from their Secret Teacher series. Does this change your opinion of teaching? Write one side of A4 exploring your response to the article.

⇨ Watch the 1995 film *Dangerous Minds*, starring Michelle Pfeiffer, and write a review.

Acknowledgements

The publisher is grateful for permission to reproduce the material in this book. While every care has been taken to trace and acknowledge copyright, the publisher tenders its apology for any accidental infringement or where copyright has proved untraceable. The publisher would be pleased to come to a suitable arrangement in any such case with the rightful owner.

Images

All images courtesy of iStock, except page 20 © Sonia Langford and page 34 © UNICEF (Flickr).

Icons on pages 12 and 36 are courtesy of Freepik.

Illustrations

Don Hatcher: pages 18 & 35. Simon Kneebone: pages 9 & 24. Angelo Madrid: pages 16 & 28.

Additional acknowledgements

Editorial on behalf of Independence Educational Publishers by Cara Acred.

With thanks to the Independence team: Mary Chapman, Sandra Dennis, Christina Hughes, Jackie Staines and Jan Sunderland.

Cara Acred

Cambridge

May 2015